Childhood Obesity

INCONTROVERSY

Other titles in the *In Controversy* series include:

Does the Death Penalty Deter Crime?
Does Illegal Immigration Harm Society?
How Should the World Respond to Global Warming?
Is Stem Cell Research Necessary?

Childhood Obesity

Bonnie Juettner

INCONTROVERSY

ReferencePoint
Press®

San Diego, CA

For more information, contact:
ReferencePoint Press, Inc.
PO Box 27779
San Diego, CA 92198
www.ReferencePointPress.com

Picture credits:
Cover: iStockphoto.com
Maury Aaseng: 43, 73
AP Images: 15, 24, 28, 60, 71, 72, 77
Landov: 11, 19, 37, 42, 55
Science Photo Library: 31, 48

LIBRARY OF CONGRESS CATALOGING-IN-PUBLICATION DATA

Juettner, Bonnie.
    Childhood obesity / by Bonnie Juettner.
        p. cm. — (In controversy series)
    Includes bibliographical references and index.
    ISBN-13: 978-1-60152-083-8 (hardcover)
    ISBN-10: 1-60152-083-2 (hardcover)
    1. Obesity in children—Juvenile literature. I. Title.
    RJ399.C6J84 2009
    618.92'398—dc22
                                                                    2009021170

Contents

Foreword

In 2008, as the U.S. economy and economies worldwide were falling into one of the worst recessions in modern history, most Americans had difficulty comprehending the complexity, magnitude, and scope of what was happening. As is often the case with a complex, controversial issue such as this historic global economic recession, looking at the problem as a whole can be overwhelming and often does not lead to understanding. One way to better comprehend such a large issue or event is to break it into smaller parts. The intricacies of global economic recession may be difficult to understand, but one can gain insight by instead beginning with an individual contributing factor such as the real estate market. When examined through a narrower lens, complex issues become clearer and easier to evaluate.

This is the idea behind ReferencePoint Press's *In Controversy* series. The series examines the complex, controversial issues of the day by breaking them into smaller pieces. Rather than looking at the stem cell research debate as a whole, a title would examine an important aspect of the debate such as *Is Stem Cell Research Necessary?* or *Is Embryonic Stem Cell Research Ethical?* By studying the central issues of the debate individually, researchers gain a more solid and focused understanding of the topic as a whole.

Each book in the series provides a clear, insightful discussion of the issues, integrating facts and a variety of contrasting opinions for a solid, balanced perspective. Personal accounts and direct quotes from academic and professional experts, advocacy groups, politicians, and others enhance the narrative. Sidebars add depth to the discussion by expanding on important ideas and events. For quick reference, a list of key facts concludes every chapter. Source notes, an annotated organizations list, bibliography, and index provide student researchers with additional tools for papers and class discussion.

The *In Controversy* series also challenges students to think critically about issues, to improve their problem-solving skills, and to sharpen their ability to form educated opinions. As President Barack Obama stated in a March 2009 speech, success in the twenty-first century will not be measurable merely by students' ability to "fill in a bubble on a test but whether they possess 21st century skills like problem-solving and critical thinking and entrepreneurship and creativity." Those who possess these skills will have a strong foundation for whatever lies ahead.

No one can know for certain what sort of world awaits today's students. What we can assume, however, is that those who are inquisitive about a wide range of issues; open-minded to divergent views; aware of bias and opinion; and able to reason, reflect, and reconsider will be best prepared for the future. As the international development organization Oxfam notes, "Today's young people will grow up to be the citizens of the future: but what that future holds for them is uncertain. We can be quite confident, however, that they will be faced with decisions about a wide range of issues on which people have differing, contradictory views. If they are to develop as global citizens all young people should have the opportunity to engage with these controversial issues."

In Controversy helps today's students better prepare for tomorrow. An understanding of the complex issues that drive our world and the ability to think critically about them are essential components of contributing, competing, and succeeding in the twenty-first century.

A Silent Epidemic

October 4, 2006, started out as a normal day for 13-year-old Jonathan Hernandez. On that day his gym class at T.W. Browne Middle School in Dallas, Texas, was running sprints, better known as "suicides." Classmate Stephanie Molina ran next to Jonathan. She was worried about him. "You could tell by his size and his body he couldn't run that much,"[1] she said later. At 5 feet 7 inches tall (170cm) and weighing 240 pounds (109kg), Jonathan was a lot heavier than most of the kids in his class. By standard measures today, he was considered extremely overweight, or obese. Jonathan did his best for about 30 minutes, but then he told Stephanie he was tired. And then he collapsed.

"The last suicide he did, that was when he hit the wall and fell," Stephanie told reporters later. "He started shaking. His eyes were white. He got brown foam coming out of his mouth . . . tears coming out from his eyes."[2]

Teachers and paramedics tried to revive Jonathan with CPR, and he was taken by ambulance to a local hospital. But he was pronounced dead a few minutes after his arrival.

Obesity and Heart Disease

No one is sure exactly why Jonathan Hernandez died. Doctors mentioned one possibility: They said that the left side of his heart might have become enlarged. (The medical term for this is *left ventricle hypertrophy.*) This condition is common in people who are obese, and by most measures, Jonathan was obese. His BMI, or body mass index, was 37.6, which means he was heavier than 99 percent of other boys his age. (BMI is a measure of weight in relation to height.)

It is not unusual for the left side of the heart to become enlarged in people who are obese. The heart has to work harder to pump blood through an obese body. The extra work causes the left side of the heart to become larger, just as exercising other muscles of the body causes those muscles to enlarge. This condition affects adults as well as children. It is especially common in extremely overweight Hispanic children and teenagers. Death from ventricle hypertrophy is rare, although young people who develop an enlarged left ventricle seem to have a higher risk of sudden death than adults with the disorder.

As little as 30 years ago in the United States, conditions like this were fairly uncommon, and obesity in children and teenagers was also not seen much. "Thirty years ago," says Nasser Hasnain, a Milwaukee pediatrician, "if you walked into a middle school, you would have two children out of a class of twenty who would be considered fat." Today, however, pediatricians more often screen children for overweight and obesity. "Now," Hasnain points out, "you can walk into a middle school class and hardly find any thin children."[3]

Gerald Hass, a Boston pediatrician, agrees. "Thirty-three years ago, when I began treating the children of the South End and Lower Roxbury, I was not confronted with 300-pound fourteen-year-olds. We worried about chicken pox and measles in children, but not Type II diabetes in teens. Now, a shocking 40 percent of our 8,000 pediatric patients . . . are clinically obese."[4]

"Thirty years ago, if you walked into a middle school, you would have two children out of a class of twenty who could be considered fat. . . . Now you can walk into a middle school class and hardly find any thin children."[3]

— Nasser Hasnain, a pediatrician in Milwaukee, Wisconsin.

Other Medical Risks

As childhood obesity increases, scientists think that heart disease, including the condition that may have killed Jonathan, will become a common pediatric disorder. Obesity increases a child's risk of high cholesterol, high blood pressure, and thickening of the arteries, all of which can lead to heart disease.

Obesity also increases a child's risk of type 2 diabetes, in which the body becomes resistant to insulin, and metabolic syndrome, in which the body simultaneously develops several different risk factors that make a young person more likely to develop heart disease or diabetes, or to have a stroke. Carrying around extra weight puts a strain on the human body. "What happens to fat people?" asks Hasnain. He continues:

> They are at higher risk for diabetes, hypertension, different kinds of cancers. And their joints break easily . . . the five foot eight body is only designed for a weight between 150 and 170 pounds. The more you carry, the more damage you do to your joints that they are not used to. Plus your heart has to pump extra to get all the blood in. You are putting a load on your heart, you are putting a load on your joints, your kidneys, everything is under a load of fat. . . . Twenty-five percent of kids who are obese will not see their sixtieth birthday.[5]

Studies show that obesity lowers a child's life expectancy by between 8 and 20 years. In one study, people who were obese as teenagers died, on average, at the age of 46.

Most of the medical risks of childhood obesity are not immediately fatal, but they can impact a child's quality of life. Obese girls usually reach puberty early, sometimes before the age of 10. Sociologists say that early puberty puts girls at risk for depression and low self-esteem, because they are teased and sometimes sexually harassed. Teenagers who are obese find that their joints hurt and they get out of breath when they run. They may also become self-conscious and easily embarrassed about their appearance. They may regard their weight as an obstacle to having an active social life. "We've never had a population like this before," says Naomi Neufeld, a pediatric endocrinologist. "Children who are overweight are 20 percent to 30 percent heavier now than they were even ten years ago. We can't even imagine the medical costs we will be seeing in the future."[6]

Losing Weight

There is one bright spot, though, in all the bad news about obesity. Children who are overweight or obese can lose weight. They are more likely than adults to make lifestyle changes and stick with them. For example, when Tom, an Orlando, Florida, 16-year-old, was a freshman in high school, he weighed 286 pounds (129.7kg)

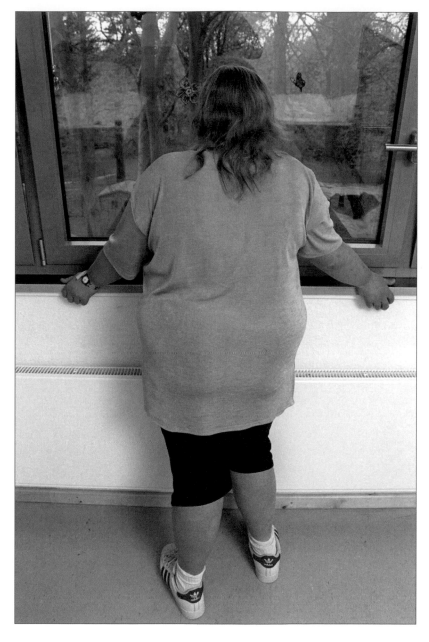

An obese 12-year-old looks out the window of a weight loss clinic that specializes in children and adolescents. Childhood obesity is rising at an alarming rate in the United States.

and had a BMI of 43.5. His doctor told him he would be dead by age 45 if he did not lose weight. His weight was making it impossible for him to try out for certain sports. He did play golf, but his golf coach, like his doctor, told him he would have to lose weight.

So Tom did. He began to be very careful about portion sizes at every meal and started eating more fruit and salads. He also set a rule for himself that he would have to be active, playing golf, baseball, racquetball, or doing weight training, on 3 days out of every 5. So far, he has lost 50 pounds (22.7kg). He now weighs 238 pounds (108kg) and has a BMI of 34. He is still losing weight. But the weight he has lost so far has given him more energy. He sleeps well at night and feels rested during the day. But it was his school's homecoming dance that really made Tom feel better. Girls kept coming up to him and complimenting him on his appearance. The experience, he says, was "a real eye-opener."[7]

It is not easy to lose weight. Children and teens cannot usually do it unless they have the support of their families. But it can be done. Once the weight drops off, most kids report that they have more energy to do the things they love to do. And their life expectancy rises more with the loss of each pound.

FACTS

- The U.S. Department of Health and Human Services has identified overweight and obesity as one of 10 major health concerns in the United States.

- In the last 20 years, childhood obesity has doubled in the United States.

- Twenty-five percent of U.S. children are overweight.

- Seventy-five percent of parents of obese children think their child's weight is normal.

- Seventy percent of obese children grow up to become obese adults.

What Are the Origins of Childhood Obesity?

I n the United States in 1965 it was rare for a child to be considered overweight. Only about 4 percent of children aged 6 to 11 and 5 percent of teenagers were overweight. At the time doctors did not even collect statistics about overweight children under age 5.

Thirty years later, in 1994, the percentages of overweight children had more than doubled. Eleven percent of children aged 6 and over were overweight. Doctors had begun to collect statistics about children from aged 2 to 5—in that age group, 7 percent were overweight. By 2006 it was not uncommon at all for a child in America to be overweight. The rate of overweight children included 12 percent of children ages 2 to 5, 17 percent of children aged 6 to 11, and 18 percent of teenagers.

During the same period, the numbers of children and teens who were not only overweight but also obese rose just as much. Although obesity is determined differently in young people than adults, the average person is considered obese if he or she is about 30 pounds (13.6kg) over ideal body weight. In 1980 about 5 percent of teenagers, 5 percent of 2- to 5-year-olds, and 7 percent of 6- to 11-year-olds were obese. By 2006 the teenage obesity rate had more than tripled. Like the teenage overweight rate, the teenage obesity rate rose to almost 18 percent. For younger children, the obesity rate, like the overweight rate, had more than doubled, rising to 12 percent for children aged 2 to 5 and to 17 percent for children aged 6 to 11. Added together, the numbers of overweight and obese kids make up 36 percent of teenagers, 34 percent of children aged 6 to 11, and 24 percent of children aged 2 to 5.

Body Mass Index

What does it mean to be overweight or obese? Most doctors define being overweight or obese as having a body mass index, or BMI, above a certain level. Body mass index is a number that measures the relationship between a person's weight and height, or the ratio of weight to height. The average, healthy adult should have a BMI between 18.5 and 24.9. An adult is defined as overweight if his or her BMI is between 25 and 29.9, and obese if his or her BMI is over 30. To have a BMI that high, an adult must be about 30 pounds (13.6kg) overweight. But BMI is measured a little differently for children and teens, because they are still growing. BMI is also measured differently for athletes, especially for bodybuilders, because they have a high proportion of muscle, which weighs more than fat. An athlete might have a high BMI and still not be overweight.

To find out whether a child's BMI is in a healthy range, a doctor consults growth charts that show what the average BMI is for children of the same age and height. To be considered overweight, a child must have a BMI that is above the eighty-fifth percentile for his or her age. To be considered obese, a child must have a BMI that is above the ninety-fifth percentile for his or her age. For example, the average 15-year-old boy is about 5 feet 7 inches tall (170cm). If he weighed 150 pounds (68kg), he would have a BMI of 23.5, and this would be considered overweight. If that same boy gained 22 pounds (10kg), his BMI would rise to 26.9, which would be considered obese. On the other hand, a 15-year-old boy who is 6 feet tall (183cm) would not be considered overweight until he reached 174 pounds (79kg). A weight gain of 24 pounds (11kg) would push him into the range of obesity.

BMI is figured differently for girls and boys. The average 15-year-old girl is about 5 feet 4 inches tall (163cm). A girl of that age and height who weighs 140 pounds (63.5kg) would have

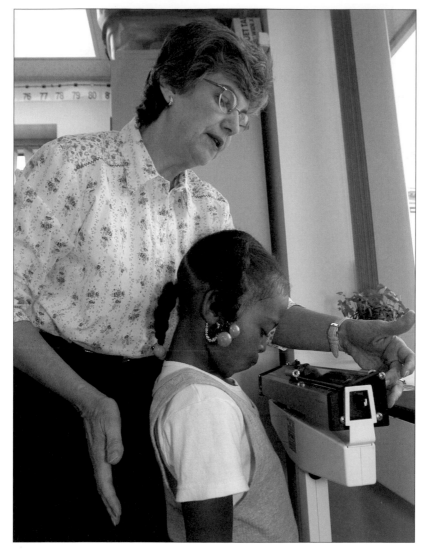

A school nurse weighs a kindergarten student to determine her body mass index. Concern about childhood obesity has prompted many school districts to add body mass index to routine student health screenings.

a BMI of 24, which would be considered overweight. If that same girl gained 24 pounds (11kg), her BMI would rise to 28.2, which would be considered obese.

Because of concerns about increasing rates of obesity, some school districts have started adding BMI screenings to the other health screenings that are routinely done at school, such as vision and hearing screenings. Some schools customarily send the results home, while others do so only if the BMI is outside a certain range. In Arkansas, BMI is recorded on student report cards along with grades. In New York, Pennsylvania, and Massachusetts,

Sleep and Obesity

Diet and exercise are not the only factors that affect a child's weight. In New Zealand researchers studied 519 children from birth to age 7. When the children reached age 7 in 2008, the researchers decided to announce their results. Children who got less than 9 hours of sleep at night were more likely to be overweight or obese. The results were the same even after the researchers compared the amount of time kids spent watching television and exercising. Children who do not get enough sleep are about 3 times more likely to become overweight or obese.

Sleep affects weight because some hormones produced by the human brain are regulated by sleep. For example, when people do not get enough sleep, their bodies produce more ghrelin—a hormone that tells the body it is hungry. When more ghrelin is produced, people feel hungrier and they eat more.

After a child gains weight, he or she may develop a disorder that makes it harder to get enough sleep—sleep apnea. During sleep apnea episodes, the sleeping body stops breathing and the sleeper wakes up for a moment. Often children or teens who have sleep apnea snore while they sleep. As a result, children who develop sleep apnea after becoming obese may end up gaining even more weight because they cannot sleep well.

several school districts screen kids, record their BMI, and send a letter home to parents.

Some kids and parents have been upset by these letters. "You're setting kids up to feel bad about how they are,"[8] says Nancy Krebs, chair of the American Academy of Pediatrics' Committee on Nutrition. Teenagers can be especially sensitive when anyone comments on their weight, whether the comment is positive or negative. Even some younger children can be susceptible to worrying about their weight. Six-year-old Karlind Dunbar stopped eating when her letter came home, even though the letter said that her BMI was normal. And some parents, like mother Christina Bové, were outraged when their children were identified as overweight based on a BMI. Moreover, she complained, schools did not tell parents what to do about it. "The school provides us with this information with no education about how to use it or what it means,"[9] she comments.

A Diet of Empty Calories

Diet is a key factor affecting a young person's weight. The issue may not be whether children and teenagers eat too much or not enough—rather, it may be whether or not they eat the right foods. Experts say the diet of most American children and teens is not very nutritious; they do not eat enough whole grains, fruits, or vegetables, while they eat more than enough white flour, potatoes, and sugar. They have replaced the nourishing foods in their diet with foods consisting mostly of empty calories. Empty-calorie foods are foods that provide energy but do not give the body the vitamins, minerals, and fiber that it needs. For example, soda, cookies, and potato chips are empty-calorie foods. They give the body calories and quick energy. But they do not give the body any vitamins or minerals, and they rarely contain any fiber. On this kind of a diet, even if a child or teen eats enough calories, he or she can still be malnourished. Even an obese or overweight child can be malnourished.

If a child responds to hunger by eating potato chips and drinking soda, he or she may gain fat but still lack the nutrients that are needed to build muscle, bone, and brain tissue. This kind of snack will leave children feeling hungry, no matter how many calories they may have just consumed, because they still have not eaten the foods that the body most needs. Often, obese and overweight children are not getting the nutrients they need. When young people (and adults) do not get enough nutrients, they tend to consume more food.

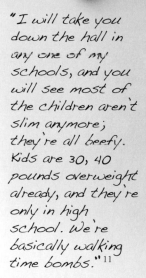

"I will take you down the hall in any one of my schools, and you will see most of the children aren't slim anymore; they're all beefy. Kids are 30, 40 pounds overweight already, and they're only in high school. We're basically walking time bombs."[11]

— School superintendent Roel Gonzalez.

Changes in Eating Habits

The types of foods that Americans eat have changed substantially since the beginning of the twentieth century. Around 1900, staying home, not going out, was considered something special for families to do together. Families were just beginning to build homes that contained a dining room. Very little of the family food budget was spent on eating out. By 2009 however, Americans were spending more than half their food budget on restaurant and cafeteria food. In 2009 about one-third of American young people between the ages of 4 and 19 were eating at least 1 fast food meal every day. Children and teenagers who eat fast food daily gain an average of 6 pounds (2.7kg) per year more than they would have gained without it.

Since the 1980s restaurants have been increasing the serving size of the foods that they serve. Fast food restaurants have increased their serving sizes the most. In 1957 the average soda served in a restaurant was 8 fluid ounces (237mL). By 2004 the average serving of soda ranged from 32 to 64 ounces (946 to 1,893 mL). In 1957 the average fast food hamburger weighed a little more than 1 ounce (28.3g). By 2004 the average burger weighed 6 ounces (170g). Young people may feel that they are so hungry that they need to eat large meals such as these. But the extra calories cause them to gain weight. Nutritionally, a better choice would be to stick with the 1957-sized 1-ounce burger, have a salad with it, and put the burger on a whole-grain bun. A meal like this would have fewer calories and be less likely to cause weight gain, and it would be more likely to assuage hunger because it would give the body the nutrients it needs.

Studies show that meals eaten at national restaurant chains are especially high in empty calories. They are much less nutritious, on average, than meals cooked at home—even if the meals cooked at home are also less than ideal. A 2008 study examined the "kid's meals" offered at 13 major restaurant chains. More than 90 percent of kid's meals at restaurants exceeded 430 calories—the number of calories that nutritionists say should be the maximum for one child's meal. The typical kid's meal at Chili's Grill and Bar,

"When I was a little girl, I played hop scotch in the school yard. I loved jumping on one foot—onesie, twosie, on and on. My brothers played dodge ball and marbles. . . . We played with sticks, dirt, kites, and water. Girls would jump rope."[12]

— Journalist Antoinette Ellis-Williams.

for example, contained more than 1,000 calories, while the typical kid's meal at Burger King contained more than 900 calories. One nutrient that nutritionists have been studying carefully is calcium. In the last 30 years, many young Americans have become deficient in calcium because they drink soda instead of milk. Soda drinking has increased by 118 percent, while milk drinking has dropped by 23 percent. Unless children are replacing milk with spinach and kale, they are probably not getting enough calcium. Some studies show that when overweight children start to get enough calcium, they tend to lose weight.

Poverty and Empty Calories

Empty-calorie foods tend to be cheaper than foods that are dense in nutrients. The difference in cost is especially noticeable if one is eating out. For example, fast food burgers and fries or fried chicken are much less expensive than a balanced meal from the buffet line at a natural foods grocery store. The price difference matters to families who are trying to care for children on a limited

Teenagers indulge in fast food at a mall in northern California. In 2009, about one-third of Americans between the ages of 4 and 19 were eating at least 1 fast food meal a day.

budget. Studies show that children who live in poverty are much more likely to become obese than children of middle- or upper-income families. They are also more likely to be malnourished. Poor families may opt for soda instead of milk to drink because it is less expensive. Doctors say that soda is the main source of sugar in children's diets.

Poor families may also choose fast food instead of a home-cooked meal because parents are working and do not have time to cook. Fast food meals are much higher in calories and lower in nutrients than home-cooked meals. Some families also choose to buy foods in bulk, which is cheaper, and store the food in a cupboard. If they do, they are less likely to buy as many fresh fruits and vegetables, because fresh fruits and vegetables rot quickly. Instead, they may buy crackers, chips, and pasta. These foods contain some nutritional value—a little bit of protein and in some cases, fiber—but they do not provide the vitamins and minerals that children need.

Pediatrician Daniel Hale works in one of the poorest counties in the nation, Starr County, Texas. He remarks, "Here in South Texas, where you can get an Extreme Gulp, which is 52 ounces of soda, and a bag of chips for a dollar . . . the kids are at great risk."[10] Roel Gonzalez, the superintendent for Rio Grande City Consolidated Independent School District, agrees. "I will take you down the hall in any one of my schools," he says, "and you will see most of the children aren't slim anymore; they're all beefy. Kids are 30, 40 pounds overweight already, and they're only in high school. We're basically walking time bombs."[11]

Physical Activity

Only a quarter of teenagers exercise regularly. This, too, has a bearing on obesity rates. According to the National Association for Sport and Physical Education, elementary-age children need at least 150 minutes, or 2½ hours, of exercise every week. Teenagers need at least 225 minutes, or almost 4 hours, of exercise weekly. Many doctors believe that children and teens need even more exercise than this. They argue that kids need at least an hour of vigorous exercise every day.

Obesity Hits a Plateau

In 2008 the rate of childhood obesity in the United States finally leveled out. This does not mean that fewer children were obese. But it does mean that the number of obese children did not rise that year.

By the time childhood obesity rates stopped rising, 32 percent of U.S. children were classified as obese. Experts were not sure what to make of the change. Some argued that parents and schools were doing a better job of making sure children ate a balanced diet and got enough exercise. Others thought that only about a third of Americans might have genes that make them prone to becoming obese—so there was always a natural limit to how high the numbers could get. Still others predicted that in the years to come, the obesity rate will not only stay level, but start to fall. David Ludwig, the director of the childhood obesity program at Boston's Children's Memorial Hospital, was hopeful. "After 25 years of extraordinarily bad news about childhood obesity," he commented, "this study provides a glimmer of hope. But it's much too soon to know whether this is a true plateau . . . or just a temporary lull."

Quoted in Tara Parker-Pope, "Hint of Hope as Child Obesity Rate Hits Plateau," *New York Times*, May 28, 2008. www.nytimes.com.

Children and teens who do not exercise may become overweight or obese even if they eat healthy food. Children who spend at least an hour moving around every day tend to burn off the calories in the food they eat. One reason why is that exercise makes kids stronger and helps them to build more muscle mass. Muscle tissue helps kids to control their weight even at times when they are not exercising. Why? All the body's tissues use energy, measured in calories. People use more calories when they are active. For example, a teen mowing the lawn uses 324 calories per hour. Playing basketball uses about 405 calories per hour. But even at rest, the body uses calories to support its functions. One of those functions is maintaining the body's tissues—keeping them alive and healthy by, for example, pumping blood in and carrying waste away. Different kinds of tissue take more calories to maintain than others, and muscle tissue takes, or burns, more calories than fat tissue does. The average teenager, even while sleeping, burns through about 45 calories per hour, but a physically fit teenager may burn more, and an obese teenager may burn less.

If young people do not exercise, they have a harder time controlling their weight. They become weaker, have less muscle mass, and have more fat tissue. So they burn fewer calories, even when they are resting, than more active kids do. As the amount of time that children spend exercising has dropped, obesity rates have risen. The bottom line, according to many experts, is that kids spend less time in physical play when they are at home, and they spend less time being active when they are at school.

Kids Spend Less Time Outdoors

In the middle of the twentieth century, young people's play was usually active. It consisted of activities such as going outside and running around or riding a bicycle. Writes Antoinette Ellis-Williams:

> When I was a little girl, I played hop scotch in the school yard. I loved jumping on one foot—onesie, twosie, on and on. My brothers played dodge ball and marbles. . . . We played with sticks, dirt, kites, and water. Girls would jump rope. . . .
>
> I could not wait for spring to go to the park with my father and fly a kite. He seemed to have more fun than we did but I loved running with the string and watching my kite sail in the spring breeze.[12]

By the late-twentieth century, though, times had changed. Parents became fearful that children playing outside unsupervised might be in danger of abduction or getting hit by a car. Most parents no longer allow children to walk or ride their bikes to school, even if the school is only a mile or two from the child's home.

Only about one-third of children who live within 1 mile (1.6km) of their school walk to it. Less than 2 percent of children who live within 2 miles (3.2km) of school ride their bikes to school.

Children today spend a lot of time playing inside, waiting until an adult has time to go outside and supervise. Teenagers, as well, spend the bulk of their time inside, doing sedentary activities. Today, many kids between the ages of 4 and 18 spend more than four hours a day playing video games, using a computer, watching videos, and watching television. "I am worried that we have lost our ability to help our children play," laments Ellis-Williams. Instead, she says, "they have computers, PDAs, video games."[13]

Some parents restrict the amount of "screen time" their kids can have. But even children whose screen time is limited still spend most of their time inside the house on sedentary pursuits. These children may read books, do arts and crafts projects, play board games, play with dolls, or build model cities. But they are still not running, jumping, and bicycling. However, several studies have shown that four hours of reading or sewing does not increase a child's risk of obesity nearly as much as four hours of television viewing does. Researchers think that this is because children tend to snack on foods with little or no nutritional value while they are watching television.

Physical Education in the Schools

By the time a teenager graduates from high school, he or she will have spent between 15,000 and 18,000 hours playing, relaxing, and having fun. In contrast, the same teen will have spent about 12,000 hours in school. Like being at home, being at school is mostly a sedentary activity for children. Except for physical education classes and recess, children and teens spend most of their time at school sitting at desks or tables.

"Younger kids have recess. In middle schools and high school physical education drops off,"[14] says Colorado state representative Alice Madden. But even in elementary schools, physical education is usually limited to once or twice a week. Many schools are

"Ten-minute recess to me is unacceptable. By the time a child gets dressed, lined up, and out the door, it will be time to come back in, not even enough time for a simple game of tag. I understand the need for. . . scores to improve, but reading, writing, and arithmetic are not the only elements of education."[16]

— Parent David McDonald.

Seventh graders at a Pennsylvania middle school cycle during a physical education class. Budget cuts have forced some school districts to cut physical education from the school day despite evidence of the importance of daily exercise.

cutting physical education even more. Meanwhile, the amount of time devoted to recess for elementary school students is also dwindling. Many schools that once offered two daily recess periods are cutting back to one or cutting minutes from the recess periods.

Most school principals understand the importance of physical education programs and regular recess breaks in the average student's day. Most teachers feel that children learn more and behave better in class when they have regular breaks for recess. But in recent years budget cuts have forced many schools to cut back on physical education programs. In 2009, for example, the Duval County School District in Jacksonville, Florida, cut out all physical education programs to meet budgetary needs. Some schools are considering eliminating physical education or recess to add more preparation time for standardized tests or to meet other academic needs.

One Colorado principal, Heidi Shriver, found that if she cut one 10-minute recess out of the school day, the saved time added up to nine extra days over the course of the school year. She could have teachers use that time to give students additional instruction or to give them more review time to prepare for standardized tests. "This is not meant to be punitive in any way," she said. "When I looked at that and weighed the time we were losing in instruction, I couldn't ignore it."[15]

In 2004 Boston elementary schools, as well, cut 10 minutes from students' combined recess/lunchtime every day. And in cold, winter weather, children lose even more of their recess time. "Ten-minute recess to me is unacceptable," parent David McDonald complained. "By the time a child gets dressed, lined up, and out the door, it will be time to come back in, not even enough time for a simple game of tag. I understand the need for . . . scores to improve, but reading, writing, and arithmetic are not the only elements of education."[16]

Lifestyle Changes

Over the last 50 years, the standard American lifestyle has changed. Families are eating out and relying on television and movies, rather than physical activity, for entertainment during their leisure hours. People also rely more on driving, rather than walking or riding bicycles, for transportation. The nutritional content of the food fed to children and teens has dropped, and kids are spending less time on physical activity.

Most doctors are not surprised, therefore, that children and teenagers are becoming more obese. Nor are they surprised when obese children turn into obese teenagers, and then into obese adults. But the extra weight obese children carry does more than follow them into adulthood. It puts a strain on their joints and makes it difficult for them to enjoy fun activities such as skating, skiing, and swimming. It puts them at risk for metabolic syndrome, heart disease, and diabetes. Eventually, it can endanger their lives.

FACTS

- A teenager living in poverty is twice as likely to be overweight as a teenager who does not live in poverty.

- A baby born in poverty in New York City has about a 25 percent chance of being obese by the age of two.

- Between 1970 and 2001, Americans doubled the amount of soda that they drank. During the same time period, the amount of milk Americans drank dropped by two-thirds.

- Between 1996 and 2007, the number of Americans who ate 2 or fewer servings of fruits and vegetables each day increased 5 percent, going from 35 percent in 1996 to 40 percent in 2007.

- Students in American elementary schools spend an average of 208 to 222 minutes per week engaged in physical activity.

- The number of teenagers taking daily physical education classes dropped by 14 percent between 1991 and 2003—from 42 percent in 1991 to 28 percent in 2003.

CHAPTER TWO

How Serious a Problem Is Childhood Obesity?

Except for his weight, doctors could not find anything wrong with Nigel Estick. At 17, Nigel was 5 feet 8 inches tall (173cm) and weighed 250 pounds (113.4kg). He had pain in his legs, his mouth was always dry, and his vision was deteriorating. Nigel was tested for leukemia, but the test came back negative. His doctors thought he might be depressed. But shortly after his test for leukemia, Nigel began vomiting 2 or 3 times a day. One morning he woke up to find that his vision was blurry. He could barely stand up. His mother took him to the emergency room at the hospital, where doctors did another blood test. This time they checked the glucose levels in Nigel's blood. (Glucose is a form of sugar.) Nigel's blood glucose levels were 8 times higher than normal. He had type 2 diabetes. He spent a week in intensive care before the glucose levels in his blood returned to normal.

Diabetes

Diabetes is the seventh leading cause of death in the United States. There are two types of diabetes, type 1 and type 2. Most young people who have diabetes have type 1, or juvenile diabetes. This is a form of the disease that has nothing to do with weight. In Type 1 diabetes, the pancreas is unable to make enough insulin, a

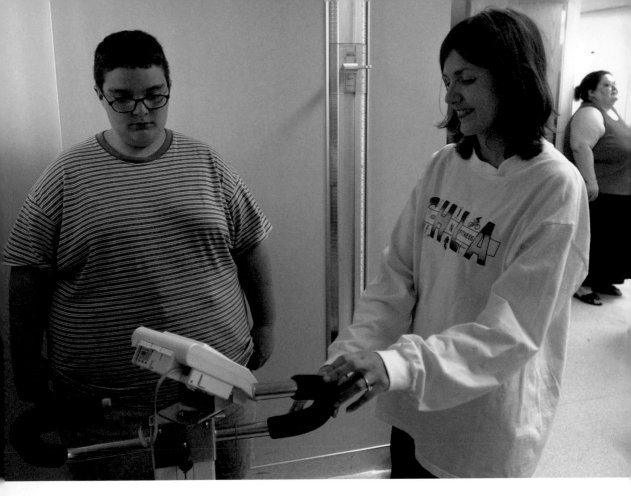

hormone that helps the body to metabolize glucose. These young people must give themselves insulin shots for the rest of their lives.

The type of diabetes Nigel contracted is different. Nigel has type 2 diabetes, which is sometimes called adult-onset diabetes. Doctors used to call it that because it was never seen in children. It is becoming common in children now. "Ten years ago, we were teaching medical students that you didn't see this disease in people under 40, and now we're seeing it in people under 10," says Robin Goland, codirector of the Naomi Berrie Diabetes Center in New York City. "With the numbers we're starting to see, this could be the beginning of an epidemic."[17]

Children are most likely to develop type 2 diabetes if they are obese. "If you want to make someone a diabetic, make them obese,"[18] says Rudolph Leibel, the Naomi Berrie center's other co-director. Doctors do not yet know exactly why obesity and diabetes are connected. They do know that when levels of glucose in the blood are high, the body releases insulin, a hormone that helps the body to process glucose and send it to the body's cells. Insulin should reduce the amount of glucose in the bloodstream. In type 1 diabetes, the pancreas cannot make enough insulin to process blood glucose. In type 2 diabetes, though, the pancreas makes plenty of insulin, but the body's cells resist its effects. This condition is called insulin resistance.

Insulin resistance develops more easily in obese people. In 2008 doctors at Temple University found a clue as to why. They discovered that the fat cells in obese people are more stressed than the fat cells in people with a healthy weight. These stressed cells produce proteins that lead to insulin resistance.

Insulin resistance is dangerous for two reasons. It causes blood glucose levels to remain high. When glucose stays in the blood, it does not reach the cells that need it for energy. At the same time, excess glucose in the blood can cause damage to a person's eyes, heart, kidneys, or nerves.

People with type 2 diabetes can control the levels of glucose in their blood with diet and exercise. Eventually, though, most type 2 diabetics need medication and insulin to control the disease. If left untreated, either type can cause blindness, poor circulation, and kidney failure. Poor circulation can cause damage to a diabetic's feet and legs—sometimes so severe that the person's toes or feet must be amputated.

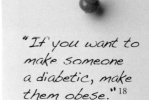

"If you want to make someone a diabetic, make them obese."[18]

— Rudolph Leibel, codirector of the Naomi Berrie Diabetes Center.

Eating a diet high in sugar does not cause type 2 diabetes to develop—at least not directly. But eating sugar and other foods that are high in empty calories can lead to obesity. Not all obese children develop diabetes, but obesity and lack of exercise increase a young person's risk of developing type 2 diabetes, particularly if other family members also have it. About 30 percent of boys and 40 percent of girls will become diabetic in their lifetimes. Type 2 diabetes is particularly common in African American and Latino families—especially families from Mexico. Nearly half of all African American and Latino children will develop diabetes in the course of their lives. It is also common in Native American, Asian American, and Pacific Islander families.

The Morbidly Obese

Children and teens with a BMI that is at or above the ninety-ninth percentile are considered morbidly obese. (Adults are classified as morbidly obese when their BMI rises to 40 or above, but the exact number has not yet been defined for children.) About 4 percent of children and teens, or 2.7 million young Americans, fall into that category. Some are more than 100 pounds (45.4kg) overweight. Carlson Rodgers, a 14-year-old living in Ossining, New York, is one of them. He weighs 362 pounds (164.2kg) and has been obese since the age of 4. "The first time I rode on a bicycle," he remembers, "the training wheels broke." In high school, he wanted to join the wrestling team. "But there was no one in my weight class," he says. "So I just came and cheered on the team."

Morbidly obese children can lose weight, but they need a lot of help and support. Carlson attended a special program at St. Mary's Rehabilitation Center for Children, in Ossining. He learned new eating habits and began to exercise. He hoped to lose enough weight to play basketball someday.

Quoted in Marek Fuchs, "County Lines: Young, Obese, and Hopeful," *New York Times*, April 28, 2002. www.nytimes.com.

Obesity's Links to Heart Disease

Diabetes is one of the biggest risks that obese children and adults face. Diabetes, however, is not the only medical risk faced by obese children. Cardiologists—doctors who specialize in heart disease—have a saying: "You're only as old as your arteries." A 2008 study showed that almost all children or teenagers who are obese or who have high cholesterol levels in their blood have artery walls that have grown as thick as those of a 45-year-old. They have atherosclerosis, which means that the flow of blood through the arteries is partially blocked by fat. Some children in the study were as young as 9 years old. Most of the children in the study not only had thickened arteries, but also had enlarged left ventricles in their hearts. Geetha Raghuveer, a University of Missouri cardiologist, cautioned that the study only involved 70 children, ranging between the ages of 9 and 16. More research is needed. But, she added, "I think this is a red flag. These kids are more similar to middle-aged adults."[19]

Atherosclerosis is a serious disorder. Doctors say that thickening of the arteries is the leading cause of death in the United States. It causes both heart attacks and strokes. About 1.2 million Americans have heart attacks every year. About 870,000 of those heart attacks turn out to be fatal. It used to be the case that heart attack patients were mostly over the age of 40. But as more children become obese, cardiologists expect to see more heart attacks happening to young adults and to adults in their 20s and 30s. Doctors are already seeing heart attacks in some children and teenagers.

Heart attacks resulting from a build-up of fats in and on the artery walls, a condition known as atherosclerosis, were once seen mainly in adults but are now also seen in young people. In this cross section of a human artery, yellow represents the fatty substance that restricts blood flow.

Metabolic Syndrome

Because of the risks of diabetes and heart disease, some doctors feel that any child with a BMI over a certain level should be tested for other diseases. Melinda Sothern, of Louisiana State University, believes any child with a BMI over the 95th percentile should be seen by a doctor. If the child has a family history of diabetes or heart disease, he or she should have blood tests to determine fasting insulin levels and glucose tolerance. Sothern states:

> Anyone above 99 percent—or more than 50 pounds overweight—should have their glucose tested and a lipid profile for cholesterol. What many people don't understand is that when a child is in the upper five percent, or more than 30 pounds overweight, he is very sick. When you do their profiles, you will find high cholesterol, high body-fat percentage, high blood pressure, risk for bone and joint disorders.[20]

One disorder that doctors feel obese children should be screened for is metabolic syndrome. In metabolic syndrome, a person develops at least three of the following five conditions: a high degree of belly fat, high blood pressure, glucose intolerance (a prediabetic condition), high triglycerides (a form of fat carried in the blood), and low "good" cholesterol (which is also called HDL cholesterol). When these symptoms appear in a cluster, they can be taken as an indication that a more serious condition, such as diabetes or heart disease, is just around the corner.

Metabolic syndrome, like heart disease and diabetes, is another disorder that used to be limited mainly to adults. But a 2008 study at the University of Miami showed that half of obese children have metabolic syndrome by the time they enter seventh grade. Some pediatricians have found it in children as young as five years old. The University of Miami researchers found these results alarming. University of Miami professor Sarah Messiah explains, "If a kid is age eight with metabolic syndrome, it will take ten years or less for that child to become a type 2 diabetic or develop heart disease."[21]

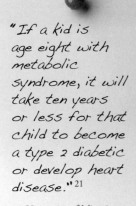

"If a kid is age eight with metabolic syndrome, it will take ten years or less for that child to become a type 2 diabetic or develop heart disease."[21]

— University of Miami professor Sarah Messiah.

When a child has metabolic syndrome by age 12, he or she may have serious heart problems by the teen years. "I am very fearful," says cardiologist John Stevens, "that in the next 10 to 20 years we will have an explosion of type 2 diabetes and coronary artery disease as these very young, very obese kids become 20-year-olds and 30-year-olds."[22]

Sore Joints and Broken Bones

Many of the medical problems facing obese children and teens are invisible during childhood. For example, teenagers may not realize they have a heart problem or are prediabetic until they become adults. But obesity can also cause more immediate health problems. Extra weight puts stress on the body's joints, especially the hips and knees. This stress can cause swelling and pain. Obese kids often find that it hurts to get out of bed in the morning or to stand up from a sitting position. Researchers have found that around 60 percent of obese children have joint pain at least once a month. Obese young people are also 30 times more likely to develop arthritis during childhood.

Obese children and teenagers are also much more likely to injure their bones or joints. The most common injury is a sprained ankle. But broken bones are also much more common in obese kids. Children whose weight is within a healthy range have a 4 percent chance of breaking a bone during their lifetimes. Among obese kids, the bone fracture rate is 13 percent. "When they fall, there's just more weight behind it,"[23] says Juni Chi-Tamai, an orthopedic surgeon at Cincinnati's Children's Hospital Medical Center. The extra weight applies more force to a bone during a fall, so the bone is more likely to snap.

Children and teens who are very obese may also develop Blount's disease, a disorder in which extra weight causes the legs to become bowed as they grow. This is what happened to 14-year-old Caleb Ezzard, who is 5 feet 4 inches tall (163cm) and weighs 362 pounds (164.2kg). Caleb used to play football, but he had to stop. "When I would run," he says, "my weight would put pressure on my leg, and my bones would start moving, and it would hurt."[24]

"I am very fearful that in the next 10 to 20 years we will have an explosion of type 2 diabetes and coronary artery disease as these very young, very obese kids become 20-year-olds and 30-year-olds."[22]

— Cardiologist John Stevens.

Early Onset of Puberty

Another way in which obesity can have an impact on a young person's daily life is that it can affect the age at which a child enters puberty. In the United States the average age of menarche, or first menstruation, for girls has been dropping for the past century.

In 1997 researchers at the University of Michigan began to track the development of 354 girls. A decade later, in 2007, they announced their results. Eighty percent of obese girls and 58 percent of overweight girls in the study group started puberty early, at age 9. But only 40 percent of healthy-weight girls did. "Our study suggests there is a link between body fat and earlier onset of puberty,"[25] observes the study's author, Joyce Lee.

Beginning puberty early is not immediately dangerous, although scientists believe it may be associated with a higher risk of breast cancer later in life. But many observers worry that it can lead to social complications and that young girls may end up in situations that they are not ready for. Amanda, a young woman recalling her experience of early puberty, says that she was teased mercilessly by other girls because she was wearing a training bra long before they were. The girls would say, "We can see your bra through your shirt," and "you dress like a tramp."[26] In response, she says, she gained more weight on purpose so that the girls would stop teasing her. Some girls are sexually harassed by men because they look older than they really are. Marcia Herman-Giddens, of the University of North Carolina at Chapel Hill, says: "Imagine being eight or nine years old and having men hit on you because you have breasts. Grown women have enough trouble dealing with unwanted sexual advances—imagine being in the fourth grade."[27]

Psychologist Diana Zuckerman of the National Research Center for Women and Families agrees. She fears that girls who hit puberty early may end up dating before they are ready or spending time with older kids who might pressure them to drink or do drugs. "We live in a culture where there is a lot of pressure on little girls to grow up too fast,"[28] she says.

"Imagine being eight or nine years old and having men hit on you because you have breasts. Grown women have enough trouble dealing with unwanted sexual advances—imagine being in the fourth grade."[27]

— Marcia Herman-Giddens, professor at the University of North Carolina at Chapel Hill.

Politics and Obesity

For some scholars, obesity is not just a health issue, but a political one. University of Colorado professor Paul Campos argues that public attacks on obesity actually target women, making them feel that they should be smaller—and less powerful—than they really are.

Kathleen LeBesco, a professor at Marymount Manhattan College, makes a similar argument about race and ethnicity. She points out that of all the cultural groups in the United States, the ones with the highest rates of obesity are African Americans and Mexican Americans. The diet industry, she says, is targeting members of these cultures, especially women. One National Heart, Lung, and Blood Institute study, she points out, actually criticizes overweight African American women for having high self-esteem and for feeling good about their bodies. This kind of argument, LeBesco claims, is racist and sexist. Many studies on diet and obesity, she argues, have a similar purpose. They are intended to make people of certain cultures feel as though they should not take up so much space in the world or as though they should try to be less visible.

Self-Esteem

Like other children, obese children who are teased or bullied may develop low self-esteem. According to the National Education Association, "For fat students, the school experience is one of ongoing prejudice, unnoticed discrimination, and almost constant harassment."[29] Students are teased, discouraged, and sometimes physically attacked. British doctor Heidi Guy says that her obese patients are teased all the time. "I would say just about all of them have been bullied or teased because of their weight," she comments. "We go through boxes and boxes of tissues and a lot of them are very tearful about everything."[30]

Often, doctors themselves discriminate against obese children. Surveys of doctors show that doctors consider their obese patients to be "weak-willed, ugly, and awkward," or "lacking in self control," or "lazy."[31] At school, teachers are less likely to identify an obese student for gifted and talented programs and more likely to identify an obese student for being at risk for learning disorders. Obese students themselves are more likely to describe themselves as lazy than they are to describe themselves as hard-working. Studies show that obese students are less likely than other students to go to college, and, if they go, their parents are less likely to pay for it.

Emily Zimmer, an eighth grader living near Seattle, told a local reporter that she tries to avoid situations that might be humiliating. For example, she was unable to go on a roller coaster because the restraints were too small for her. "It was just so embarrassing," she said. "What if somebody I knew had seen that happen?" As she gets older, Emily finds she is teased less. "People are respecting me more because they realize I'm not just fat; I'm a human being. I have talent, I have a 4.0 grade average, and I play a musical instrument, for crying out loud. I hope that impresses them a little bit."[32]

Sarah, an obese 15-year-old living in Britain, reports being not only teased, but physically bullied and attacked, because of her weight. Sarah says: "I left school three years ago because I was being badly bullied. I had pushing and shoving, people calling names, like 'fat cow' and had eggs thrown at me. . . . I get picked on because I'm not wearing fashionable clothes. I get picked on because of the shops I go to and it makes me really upset and I feel sick and angry all the time."[33]

Matt, an eighth grader, was also attacked because of his weight. Although only 13, he weighed 260 pounds (117.9kg) and was 6 feet tall (183cm). Like many obese teenagers, he seemed older than his age and felt comfortable interacting with adults. Kids his own age, though, viewed him as a target. Matt writes:

> I guess it's like a passage of honor for some of the wrestlers to tackle me. They'll come at me in herds, and one of them

"People are respecting me more because they realize I'm not just fat; I'm a human being. I have talent, I have a 4.0 grade average, and I play a musical instrument, for crying out loud. I hope that impresses them a little bit."[32]

— Emily Zimmer, Seattle eighth grader.

will ask me if I want to wrestle. I usually refuse. I'll turn around to walk away, and they'll hit me. Then I'll turn around and say, "Fine. I'll take you down." Then they'll get in this weird wrestling stance and they'll jump at me and tackle my legs. I'll end up falling on the ground, and they'll try to grab my neck. . . . The group would circulate through people so they always had a person that wasn't so tired to try to wear me down.[34]

In Charlottesville, North Carolina, two guidance counselors, frustrated with the low self-esteem they saw in many overweight students, created a club for obese girls. They called it the Bold and Beautiful Club. The girls in the club were all fifth and sixth graders, but many looked older because they had reached puberty early. Each meeting of the club starts with exercise, such as walking, dancing, or aerobics. Then there is a lesson on nutrition, personal health, or hygiene. The club organizers make sure to include topics that they think will be of high interest to the girls, such as how to give a facial. They do not have the girls weigh themselves

Students in Florida move to an interactive video game. Dancing, walking, and aerobics are among the types of fun and low-impact exercise that young people with weight problems are encouraged to do.

and do not push them to diet. Instead, they focus on providing emotional support and building the girls' self-esteem.

The American Obsession with Weight

Many critics argue that obese children's struggle with low self-esteem is caused by the American obsession with weight. Americans obsess about obesity, they say, not because it is dangerous or unhealthy, but because in our culture it is considered ugly. "We are in a moral panic about obesity,"[35] says Sander Gilman of the University of Illinois at Chicago. Gilman feels that obese children and teens are often treated as though they were lazy or as if they had no willpower or self-control. People with other health problems are not usually accused of laziness or self-indulgence, but obese people face these accusations all the time.

Paul Campos, a scholar at the University of Colorado, agrees, and he goes on to point out that many overweight people are perfectly healthy. "Contrary to almost everything you have heard," he argues, "weight is not a good predictor of health. In fact a moderately active larger person is likely to be far healthier than someone who is svelte but sedentary."[36] Gilman and Campos do not dispute the statistics that connect obesity with heart disease, diabetes, and other medical risks. They believe the health risks of obesity are associated with malnutrition and lack of exercise rather than too much weight. Campos believes that exercise makes a much greater difference in a person's health than weight does. An obese person who exercises regularly, he feels, could avoid many of the health risks that other obese people face. As a result, although Campos and Gilman disagree with many doctors about the risks of obesity, they still make the same recommendations that doctors do—they advise children and teens to exercise regularly and eat well.

> "Contrary to almost everything you have heard, weight is not a good predictor of health. In fact a moderately active larger person is likely to be far healthier than someone who is svelte but sedentary."[36]
>
> — Paul Campos, professor at the University of Colorado.

Obesity Puts Kids at Risk

Overall, doctors and researchers agree—obesity is associated with serious health risks. Children and teens who are obese are at a much higher risk of entering puberty early and of developing heart disease, type 2 diabetes, metabolic syndrome, and joint problems. Not all doctors agree about whether obesity is a direct cause of these health problems. But they do know that reducing obesity can, directly or indirectly, prevent these problems.

Doctors are very hopeful about their ability to help young people who are overweight and obese. Obese children and teens, unlike obese adults, have the chance to try to lose weight before the damage to their health is permanent. And, unlike adults, they are motivated—they usually want to be able to play basketball or ice skate or go bicycling with friends. Recovery from childhood obesity is possible—with some education from doctors and support from one's family.

FACTS

- About 7 percent of obese children aged 5 to 17 have at least 1 risk factor for heart disease. About 39 percent of obese children have 2 or more risk factors.

- Among obese children and teens, 61 percent have at least one additional risk factor for heart disease, such as high blood pressure or high cholesterol.

- Between 2004 and 2007, the number of U.S. children taking medication to control diabetes and high blood pressure rose by 15 percent.

- Doctors hypothesize that by 2035, 100,000 kids who are obese today will have developed heart disease as adults.

- By the time they reach the ages of 12 to 14, half of obese children have developed metabolic syndrome.

CHAPTER THREE

What Are the Causes of Childhood Obesity?

Numerous studies document the connection between diet, lack of exercise, and obesity. But individual people do not always see the connection between what they eat, how much physical activity they have in their life, and how much they weigh. Francine Kaufman, a pediatric endocrinologist at Children's Hospital in Los Angeles, says, "When we sit those families and children down and explain to them, it's like we turned on a light." She continues: "You know, you think, you go to McDonald's, it's a nice place; get a couple of Happy Meals and some of these now super size meals. . . . I think some of our families are just glad to be able to feed their families. They don't understand that that meal is laden with fat and overburdened with calories and not the best thing to eat."[37]

Words like this fill obese young people and their families with hope. They begin to feel that it is possible to lose weight, if they eat a healthy diet and get enough exercise. And they are right, up to a point—studies show that focusing on diet and exercise is good advice. However, scientists are discovering that the causes of obesity are more complex than this. It really is harder for some children to control their weight than it is for others—no matter what they eat.

Genes and Obesity

Doctors believe that weight is strongly influenced by genes, or DNA—the unique characteristics that children inherit from their parents. About 75 percent of the variation in people's weights is thought to be caused by their genes. This means that weight is one of the most strongly inherited conditions. Genes are an even more important factor in weight gain and weight loss than they are in other inherited conditions, such as mental illness, breast cancer, and heart disease. This does not mean that a child of obese parents will automatically become obese, just as the child of a parent who has cancer is not automatically going to develop cancer. It just means that a child of obese parents is at higher risk for obesity than the child of thin parents.

Twins Studies

Scientists studying obesity have taken a keen interest in twins, especially identical twins. Identical twins do not have identical DNA. But their DNA is a very close match to each other. Researchers who are interested in obesity began to wonder whether identical twins who were adopted and raised by different parents would develop physically in similar ways. They wondered whether twins who were separated would end up with similar weights, or whether they would differ depending on whether the adoptive family fed them a healthy diet or encouraged them to exercise.

When they began to study identical twins, researchers found that the BMI of twins tends to be about the same, whether they are separated at birth or grow up together. This makes doctors think that genes play an important role in regulating weight. Otherwise, eating different food and getting different amounts of exercise ought to result in children having different weights and different BMIs.

Researchers moved on from studying identical twins to studying other adopted children, including nontwins. Scientists found that 80 percent of children with obese birth parents end up becoming obese themselves—even if they are fed a healthy, low-fat

"You think, you go to McDonald's, it's a nice place; get a couple of Happy Meals and some of these now super size meals. . . . They don't understand that that meal is laden with fat and overburdened with calories and not the best thing to eat."[37]

— Francine Kaufman, pediatric endocrinologist at Children's Hospital Los Angeles.

Obesity tends to run in families, as can be seen in this photograph of a family relaxing on a park bench. Experts believe that genes have a strong influence on weight, although lifestyle also plays a role.

diet by their adoptive parents. This made doctors even more certain that genes are an important factor affecting weight gain.

Genes and Environment

Doctors have suspected a genetic role in obesity for decades. In the late 1990s geneticists identified 5 different genes that are related to obesity. But those 5 genes are rare and probably account for less than 10 percent of obesity cases. Then in 2006 a team of scientists at Boston University discovered a more common gene for obesity. The gene, called Insig2, is found in about 10 percent of people of European or African descent. Now, investigators are studying at least 60 genes that are suspected of causing obesity. Some scientists think that as many as 100 genes may be involved.

Once researchers learned about the strong connection between genes and weight, they were left with a puzzle. Childhood obesity rates in the United States have skyrocketed in the last 30 years. But the gene pool—the complete set of genes that exists among Americans—has not changed that much during the same period. Genes cannot be responsible for the entire increase

Three Snapshots of Obesity Among U.S. Adults

Obesity among U.S. adults rose dramatically between 1990 and 2007, public health experts fear that the growing rate of childhood obesity will inevitably lead to increases in adult obesity. In 1990, the prevalence of obesity was less than 15 percent in all states. By 1998, 7 states had a prevalence of obesity between 20 and 24 percent but no states exceeded that rate. In 2007, only one state (Colorado) had a prevalence of obesity less than 20 percent, 30 states had a prevalence of at least 25 percent, and 3 of these states (Alabama, Mississippi, and Tennessee) had a prevalence of at least 30 percent.

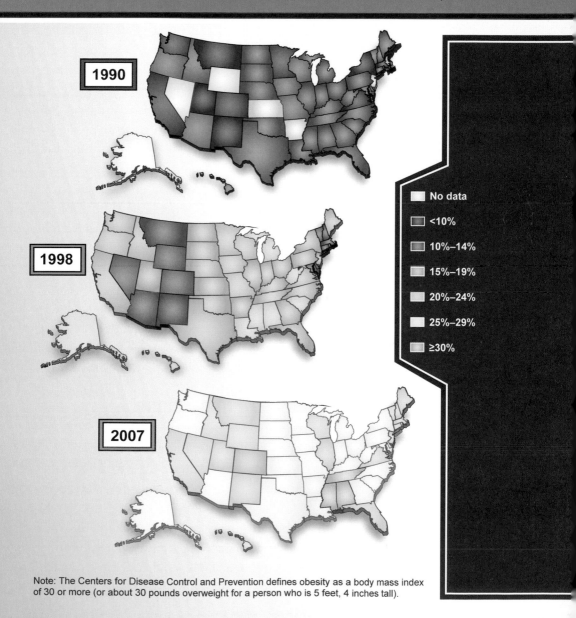

1990

1998

2007

No data
<10%
10%–14%
15%–19%
20%–24%
25%–29%
≥30%

Note: The Centers for Disease Control and Prevention defines obesity as a body mass index of 30 or more (or about 30 pounds overweight for a person who is 5 feet, 4 inches tall).

Source: Centers for Disease Control and Prevention, "CDC Behavioral Risk Factor Surveillance System," 2009. www.cdc.gov.

in obesity. Scientists have concluded that although genes may be responsible for 75 percent of weight variation, the remaining 25 percent can also be quite significant. A child who is genetically susceptible to becoming obese may or may not actually do so. A child's environment, culture, family, and personal behavior can also make a difference. The child of obese parents might not become obese if he or she grows up eating mostly fruit and vegetables and exercises regularly. But the same child might become obese growing up in a family that eats mostly junk food. Researcher Susan Carnell says that genes may affect appetite more than weight itself. "So while one child might be perfectly okay living in a home filled with [potato chips] and cake," she says, "another might find it very challenging."[38]

Geneticist Rudy Leibel explains it this way. Suppose that 100 people were exposed to a famine. They would all begin to starve, losing weight and becoming thin. But not all 100 would become equally thin. Some would lose more weight than others, even if they all ate an equally small amount of food. Likewise, if all 100 people feasted on a large amount of food, they might all gain weight, but each person would gain a different amount. The fact that the people lost or gained weight is based on the food they ate and the amount of exercise they got. But the exact amount of weight that was gained or lost is controlled by genes. This is why some people think they can gain weight even if they just look at cake or ice cream, while others seem to be able to eat anything they want and never gain weight.

"While one child might be perfectly okay living in a home filled with [potato chips] and cake, another might find it very challenging."[38]

— Researcher Susan Carnell.

Obesity Among the Pima People

Certain ethnic groups have very high obesity rates. One of these groups is the Akimel O'odham, or Pima, a Native American nation of southern Arizona. The Pima have higher obesity rates than almost any other group in the world. (Only a few Pacific Islander nations have more obesity than the Pima.)

Many Pima babies begin to gain extra weight in their first month of life. Pima children gain much more weight than average and have higher-than-average BMIs, especially from birth to age 11. Pima children are four times more likely to be obese than the

The Set Point

Neurologist Barry Levin says that a person's weight tends to return to a set point, the weight that the body naturally tries to maintain. Some people have genes that make them more likely to have a set point that is higher, while other people are genetically likely to have a lower set point. No matter what a person's set point is, it will tend to go up over time. The set point goes up whenever a person gains weight and stays at the higher weight for a period of time. In young people the set point rises constantly, as children gradually grow, develop, and gain weight. However, the set point cannot fall, even if an obese person loses a lot of weight and stays at the lower weight for a long time.

This means that people who have lost weight—whether they have lost a lot of weight or a little weight—find it very difficult to keep the weight off. Their bodies naturally want to return to the last set point. As a result, people who once were obese but have lost weight must eat less, even if they weigh the same amount, than people who never were obese. Unfortunately, the change in the body's set point is permanent. Formerly obese people are likely to gain back the weight they lost. Not all gain their weight back—but those who manage to stay thin are likely to be hungry often.

average American child, and half develop diabetes at some point in their lifetimes.

Scientists believe that obesity rates among the Pima have to do with genes that evolved over the course of the 2,000 years that they have lived in the Arizona desert. During most of that time, they lived as farmers. But the desert is a harsh and difficult environment in which to farm, and there were frequent famines. Geneticists believe the Pima evolved a "thrifty gene" that enabled them to store a lot of fat during good times, when there was plenty of food, so that they could use the stored fat to survive during periods of famine. When an ethnic group has thousands of years of regular famines in its history, scientists hypothesize, it is much more likely to evolve genes that lead to obesity when the famines have become a thing of the past.

The thrifty gene does not mean that all Pima will automatically be obese. Researchers say that some Pima manage to control their weight and avoid diabetes by exercising and watching their diet. Researchers have seen this in a group of Pima who live in a remote mountain area of Mexico. Members of this group live by subsistence farming. This means that they grow and eat their own vegetables and grains. They do not eat very much processed food from a grocery store. Although they have essentially the same genes as the Arizona Pima, the Mexican Pima do not have high rates of obesity or diabetes. They eat much more healthfully than the Arizona Pima, and they get a lot more exercise through their daily activities.

How Behavior Affects Obesity

Although scientists are fascinated by what they are learning about possible links between genes and obesity, many doctors still feel strongly that lifestyle influences obesity. They point to the difference between the Arizona and Mexican Pima and argue that children who eat healthfully and get plenty of exercise should be able to control their weight, even if they possess one of the genes linked to obesity. Wondering if this were so, in 2008 sociologist Molly Martin from the University of Pennsylvania decided to do another twins study. She used data collected by nationwide studies in the late 1990s. Martin discovered that genes do control a child's tendency to gain or not gain weight in different contexts. But she found that family behavior makes a big difference, too.

"We had a gut sense that this . . . was true," she said. "But in the research literature it actually had not been proven." Martin felt that geneticists had focused too much on genes. She wanted to include family behavior as a variable in her study. When she did, her results showed that eating regular meals and limiting screen time—time spent watching television, using computers, or playing video games—could be effective in reducing obesity rates. These behavior changes even reduced obesity in families that had a genetic tendency to become obese. "I think that if we find little things on a daily basis," she wrote, "like going for walks, playing with the dog, maybe going sledding this winter, those little things actually do matter."[39]

Watching Too Much Television

There is one piece of family behavior that all researchers agree contributes to childhood obesity—watching television. Scientists have been studying the effect of television on children's health for more than 30 years. Studies show that television has a bigger impact on a child's weight than diet or exercise. Many teenagers and children over the age of 8 spend more than 8 hours a day watching television. Younger children spend between 2 and 3 hours a day watching television. By the time children start middle school, more than half sleep with a television in their bedroom. All of this time spent in front of a television increases the likelihood of a child gaining weight or becoming obese. A child who watches television after school, for example, is not outside climbing trees, skateboarding, bicycling, or jumping rope.

In a 2006 study, researchers gave people pedometers to measure the number of steps they took each day. They also recorded the number of hours of television each person in the study watched. The study showed that for each hour of television a person watched, he or she took 144 fewer steps during the day. People who watched 4 hours of television per day were unlikely to take 10,000 steps a day—the number of steps experts agree is the minimum necessary for a person to be physically fit.

Another part of the link between television and weight gain is the commercials. Between television shows, kids are likely to see ads for food, which makes them hungry. A 2007 study showed that obese children's appetites increased by 134 percent after watching food commercials. Overweight children's appetites increased by 101 percent after the commercials, while the appetites of children of normal weight increased by 84 percent.

"If we find little things on a daily basis, like going for walks, playing with the dog, maybe going sledding this winter, those little things actually do matter."[39]

— Sociologist Molly Martin of the University of Pennsylvania.

Children who sit and read books after school, like the television watchers, are not being physically active either, but they are much less likely to gain weight than the television watchers because there are no food advertisements inside books.

The more television they watch, the heavier children and teens tend to be. But reducing television time is one of the hardest lifestyle changes for families to make. Leonard Epstein, the director of a Buffalo, New York, treatment center for obese children, says: "We've not had any success when we talk about getting TVs out of kids' bedrooms. We've had absolutely no success in reducing the number of TVs in homes. We tell parents, turn the TV toward the wall, or put hard-backed chairs in front of the TV. . . . People just don't want to do that."[40]

Researchers find family resistance to reducing television time extremely frustrating. "You don't put a gun in a room where a kid sleeps," argues Harvard School of Public Health researcher Steven Gortmaker. "You don't put a refrigerator in a room where a kid sleeps. You don't put a TV in a room where a kid sleeps."[41]

Researchers have not studied other forms of screen time, such as using a computer or playing video games, as much as they have studied television. But early studies of video game and computer use seem to indicate that they, too, are associated with an increased risk of obesity.

Emotional Eating

Even though it adds to obesity, many people feel that eating in front of a television can also be a comfort. Teenagers may snack in front of a television for a long time without ever really being hungry. Studies show that teenagers also eat at other times when they are not hungry. They may eat at parties as a way to cope with nervousness. Sometimes they eat because they are bored.

Snacking to cope with stress or to unwind after a rough day is called emotional eating. It is eating that happens because a person needs comfort, not because he or she is hungry. This kind of eating is something people do to improve their mood. "We've known for a long time that adults eat for emotional reasons," says nutritionist Lorraine Mongiello, who works at St. Charles Hospital in Port Jefferson, New York. "We now are beginning to understand that children do, too. Kids eat because they are bored or sad or angry."[42] Young people may use food in the same way that adults use coffee—to help them to become more alert in the middle of the afternoon, or to help them to feel more positive and energetic. They may turn to something sweet to help them feel better after a bad day.

Sometimes teenagers use food to try to soothe strong feelings, like depression, anxiety, anger, and loneliness. A 2008 study showed that teenage girls eat more if they think they are not popular—and that comfort eating usually causes a weight gain of about 11 pounds (5kg). But comfort eating can get out of control and cause even larger weight gains.

> *"We tell parents, turn the TV toward the wall, or put hard-backed chairs in front of the TV. . . . People just don't want to do that."*[40]
>
> — Leonard Epstein, director of a Buffalo, New York, treatment center for obese children.

Exposure to Toxins

Diet, genetics, and exercise are important factors affecting a child's weight. But in recent years, scientists have discovered other factors. Some scientists have begun to think that exposure to certain chemicals can make a child more likely to become obese. In 2009 researchers at Mount Sinai Medical Center in New York City completed a study on chemicals in plastic. They studied a group of girls in East Harlem, in New York City. They were trying to find out if the girls had been exposed to phthalates—a chemical that is used in plastic and in personal care products. Phthalates are in many common everyday objects. They are in plastic toys, pacifiers, and vinyl siding used on houses. They are also in certain kinds of makeup and nail polish.

To find out if children had been exposed to phthalates, researchers took urine samples. They tested the urine for phthalate concentration. "The heaviest girls have the highest concentrations of phthalates metabolites in their urine," explained researcher Philip Landrigan. "It goes up as the children get heavier, but it's most evident in the heaviest children. . . . We don't know if it's cause and effect or an accidental finding."[43] Researchers are not sure yet whether the connection between the phthalates and obesity is real. To find out more, they will do a national study, looking at more kids and more variables.

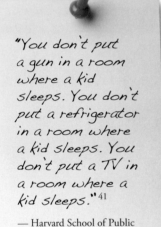

"You don't put a gun in a room where a kid sleeps. You don't put a refrigerator in a room where a kid sleeps. You don't put a TV in a room where a kid sleeps."[41]

— Harvard School of Public Health researcher Steven Gortmaker.

A Possible Virus Connection

Most research into the causes of obesity has focused on genes, families, and lifestyles. Nikhil Dhurandar, an epidemiologist at Wayne State University in Detroit, has studied another possibility. In the 1980s Dhurandar practiced medicine in India. He noticed that he was finding antibodies to a particular virus in the blood of some of his heavier-than-average patients. (Antibodies are specialized proteins that the body produces when it is fighting off a disease.) He wondered if the virus could make it harder for children to stay at a healthy weight. When he moved to the United States, Dhurandar did several studies in which he injected the virus into chickens and mice. The

Pacific Islanders

Pacific Islanders are the only ethnic group in the world to have higher obesity rates than the Pima. Scientists think that in their history, Pacific Islanders had to go without food for long periods of time in order to make long canoe trips from one island to another. As a result, they, like the Pima, evolved a "thrifty gene"—a gene that helps them to be very efficient in how they use food calories. Like the Pima, Pacific Islanders also have high rates of diabetes, and they develop diabetes at lower weights than other ethnic groups do.

infected chickens and mice gained two-thirds more weight than uninfected animals did.

In the 1990s Dhurandar turned to human studies. He took blood samples from obese patients and checked to see if they had been exposed to the virus. He found that 1 out of 3 obese Americans had antibodies to the virus in their blood. But only 1 out of 20 slimmer Americans did. Then Dhurandar did his own twins study in the late 1990s. Twins usually weigh about the same. But Dhurandar found 90 pairs of identical twins in which one twin weighed significantly more than the other. When he tested their blood, he discovered that in cases where one twin tested positive for an antibody to the virus and the other did not, the twin who tested positive always weighed more and had more body fat than the twin who tested negative. Dhurandar's study was not conclusive. It suggests a link between viruses and obesity, but more studies are needed before researchers can be sure that there is a connection.

Causes Differ from Person to Person

The causes of obesity may differ from one person to the next. Many children and teens come from families that have a genetic tendency to gain weight easily. If those same children eat a diet that relies too much on empty calories and do not get enough exercise, they can easily become obese. They may have a hard time losing those extra pounds when they try to do so. On the other hand, even children and teens who have no genetic tendency to gain weight will still put on weight if they spend too much time watching television and too little time exercising and if they eat too much junk food.

FACTS

- If one parent is obese, a child has a one in three chance of being obese as well.

- One of the newly discovered obesity genes is called FTO. Having 1 FTO gene makes a person 30 percent more likely to be obese. Having 2 FTO genes makes a person 70 percent more likely to be obese.

- Huge portion sizes, especially of fast food, have been linked to obesity. The average fast food burger has grown six times larger and the average serving of soda has quadrupled in size in the last few decades.

- Since 1977, the number of young people walking or biking to school has dropped 40 percent—children who used to walk or bike are being driven to school or are riding a bus instead.

Can Childhood Obesity Be Reversed?

When Bruce, who is an African American teenager, was 18, his pediatrician told him that he had high blood pressure and urged him to lose weight. Obesity runs in Bruce's grandfather's family, so his mother, Lottie, was worried. She feared that Bruce would have lifelong health problems if a change was not made. So she made the change. She took Bruce to a Charlottesville, Virginia, weight loss clinic and asked for advice.

First, Lottie got rid of her tall glasses and bought short ones that hold only 8 ounces of fluid (0.24L). She also bought plates that were divided into three sections and set a rule for her family that the biggest section was always reserved for vegetables. She changed her shopping and cooking habits, working to make sure that she bought foods that were low in fat and high in nutrients.

Meanwhile, Bruce's dietician gave him a pedometer to clip onto his belt. The pedometer counted Bruce's footsteps to help him keep track of how much walking he was doing each day. He set a goal of walking at least 7,000 steps every day. To accomplish that, he began walking up and down the stairs during commercials when he was watching television. He started shooting baskets at the hoop up the street with his sister, LaToya. And he and his mother and siblings began walking around a local track regularly.

Gradual Weight Loss

During the first month of this system, Bruce lost 6 pounds (2.7kg). His mother and siblings lost weight, too. They all lost fat and added muscle. Bruce's blood pressure has dropped. And he has much more energy than he used to have. So far, Bruce's story is a success. How did he manage to do what so many obese children and adults find so difficult?

Bruce's weight loss program went about as smoothly as it could. He had the support of his mother, who customized his plan for him. She and his siblings changed their eating habits right along with him. He included regular exercise in his daily routine. And he concentrated on eating foods that were nutritious—foods that are high in vitamins, minerals, and protein. Eating nutritious food helped Bruce because it reduced his appetite and gave his body the building blocks it needed to continue to grow and develop.

Bruce's story, like that of so many other teens, shows that reversing obesity is possible. Eating a good diet and getting exercise do work. However, children and teens, like adults, often gain back lost weight. It does not happen because they lose interest in eating healthfully or stop enjoying exercise. Rather, what usually happens is that they get busy. Bruce might have final exams to study for. He might get a job after school. If something happens to take up a lot of his time or make him tired, he might not have the energy to prepare healthy meals, and he might start to rely more on convenience foods again. He might not manage to make time to walk around the track or shoot hoops with his sister. If that happens, the weight that he lost could start to creep back on. If he hopes to keep his weight down for the rest of his life, he will have to stay vigilant, making time to take care of his health.

"Adult programs don't work for kids."[44]

— Karen Miller-Kovach, chief science officer at Weight Watchers.

Weight Loss Programs

It can be hard to find a weight loss program that specializes in children. If children follow an adult program, the recommended diet may not provide enough nutrients for a growing child. "Adult programs don't work for kids,"[44] says Karen Miller-Kovach, the chief science officer at Weight Watchers. Parents usually take one of two approaches to helping their obese children lose weight. Either they make lifestyle changes at home, the way Bruce's mother

did, or they send the child to a residential weight loss program, or camp. Neither approach is an easy solution.

Parents often send their children to a weight loss camp if they are not sure how to provide the support a child will need to lose weight. Parents may not know how to cook nutritious meals, for example. But eventually, a child who loses weight at camp must come home and continue to eat healthfully and exercise. Experts say that the entire family will have to support the child's efforts. According to weight loss camp counselor Lydia Burton, parents need education just as much as their children do. She explains:

> There are seminars for parents, but a lot of parents don't show up, so the kids go back to the exact same situations. They learn a little bit from camp, but the parents

Teenagers select foods for breakfast at a weight loss clinic for obese youth. Participants at extended-stay camps and clinics learn about exercise and diet but keeping up what they learn is a challenge once they return home.

still continue to feed them the way they have been. After camp ends the child either gains it back or the kid leaves with an intense fear of food. A couple have told me that they're afraid of food and they're afraid of overeating . . . it's a borderline eating disorder.[45]

The camp approach can often be more effective when parents go with children to camp. Parents of obese children are often obese themselves. If they go to a weight loss camp with their children, they can learn about nutrition, too. Then they can offer more nutritious meals when they return home. Mary Stevens is one parent who went with her son to camp. "I didn't want my son to feel as if my husband and I were sending him away because something was wrong,"[46] she explained, and notes that she wanted to lose weight, too. At the time Stevens weighed 192 pounds (87kg) and was 5 feet 2 inches tall (157.5cm). Her 14-year-old son weighed 235 pounds (106.6kg). At camp, she lost 38 pounds (17.2kg); her son lost 47 pounds (21.3kg). They were able to keep most of that weight off during the winter and returned to camp the following summer to try to lose more.

Outpatient Programs

Weight loss camps are expensive—a weeklong stay can cost more than a thousand dollars—and it takes about six weeks to start to see a difference. So, for many people, camps like these are not an option. A more affordable solution is a hospital program. Many hospitals offer free outpatient weight loss programs. Kids can meet once a week with a doctor, counselor, and nutritionist. Some programs include exercise classes.

Fourteen-year-old Carlson Rodgers attended the outpatient program at St. Mary's Rehabilitation Center for Children in Ossining, New York. Weighing 362 pounds (164.2kg) at age 14, he had been overweight since before the age of 4. He was losing weight, but slowly. Carlson says he has learned to make better dietary choices since attending the program at St. Mary's. "I used to eat a lot of McDonald's and Burger King and Taco Bell and Pizza Hut and Wendy's," he confides. "Now I've learned to have cold cuts, tomato and vegetables."[47]

Keeping Weight Off

There is a physiological reason why it is so hard for obese people to lose weight. When obese people go on a diet, their bodies begin to starve and their metabolic rate drops. The metabolic rate is the rate at which a person's body converts stored fat into energy. When the body begins to starve, it stops burning as many calories as it did before. Instead, starving bodies burn about 24 percent fewer calories than they did before the diet began. A body will naturally want to revert to its set point—the weight it was at before the dieting started.

Researchers also found that thin people who try to gain weight cannot keep the weight on. Thin people trying to gain weight do not begin to starve, but their bodies still seem to return to a set point.

The starvation that obese people go through when they diet explains why so many tend to hoard food. The process of starvation can affect the brain. It causes dieters to have fantasies about food and take it everywhere.

Ten-year-old Melanie also attended a weekly outpatient program. Melanie was not obese yet, but she was overweight, and her doctor feared she might become obese. After Melanie started attending the program, she began to make different choices about what to eat. She would choose a salad instead of a hamburger, or an ice cream cone instead of a hot fudge sundae. "At night when I watch television," she says proudly, "instead of getting a chocolate-covered granola bar, I get an apple."[48]

Studies show that outpatient programs can be very effective in helping most obese young people to lose weight, as long as they remain in the program. Once teens leave their weight loss programs—whether the program is a residential camp or a weekly outpatient class—they usually regain the weight that they previously lost. To help overcome this problem, some hospitals offer a weekly follow-up, or weight loss maintenance classes. Young people who attend weekly maintenance classes are more likely to maintain their weight at the same level as when they completed the program.

Developing Healthy Eating Habits

Every weight loss program starts with education about healthy eating habits. Even when children and teens do not go to a program, and instead decide to make lifestyle changes on their own, experts recommend that families at least make time to see a doctor and a nutritionist or dietician. Getting nutritional advice is important, because some weight loss diets can be dangerous for kids.

The basic principle behind the weight loss diets used by adults is to take in fewer calories than the body uses. If the body gets fewer calories than it needs to function, it will have to get those calories by using the energy stored in fat cells. Adults who are obese can often lose weight by following a calorie counting approach. However, for young people, losing weight is not as simple as just restricting calories. Dieticians say that children and teenagers should not restrict their calorie consumption too much, because they need calories for healthy growth.

Instead, most of the diets that doctors recommend to kids have one idea in common—the foods that young people eat should be dense in nutrients. Many weight loss programs for kids use the "traffic light" diet. They classify foods that are high in fat and calories but low in nutrients as red lights. Red lights include foods such as cheeseburgers, chicken nuggets, soda, and ice cream. Red light foods should only be eaten rarely. Cheese, tortilla chips, crackers, white rice, and other foods that have some nutritional value but also are low in fiber and/or high in fat are yellow lights. Yellow light foods can be eaten frequently but in moderate portion sizes. Vegetables, beans, whole grains, lean meats, and water get a green light—kids can eat unlimited amounts of green light foods. The goal is to get kids "down to about seven red lights per week," says pediatrician

"I used to eat a lot of McDonald's and Burger King and Taco Bell and Pizza Hut and Wendy's. Now I've learned to have cold cuts, tomato and vegetables." [47]

— 14-year-old Carlson Rodgers.

Thomas Robinson, who directs the Center for Healthy Weight at the Lucille Packard Children's Hospital in Stanford, California.

At the Lucille Packard Children's Hospital program, nutritionists also take time to educate young people about the contents of red light foods. "We have a worksheet that outlines how many teaspoons of fat are in certain foods," says nutritionist Cindy Zedeck. "For example, maybe a hamburger at a fast food place would have about six to eight spoons of fat. We have kids scoop out spoons of Crisco and put it on a plate. Then they can really see how much fat they're consuming when they eat that hamburger."[49]

Studies show that the traffic light system works well for kids. Ten years after beginning the traffic light diet, most children and teens are still following it and have not regained the weight that they previously lost.

Nutrition for Growing Bodies

One advantage of the traffic light system is that it does not deprive kids of food. Instead, it emphasizes eating foods that are nutritious. Young people need plenty of nutrients in their diets, even if they are overweight or obese, because they are growing taller, adding bone length and bone density, and because their brains are going through a dramatic phase of development.

Neuroscientist Jay Giedd of the National Institute of Mental Health explains why: The teen years are the time when the brain prunes itself, setting up the connections that it will need later in life for planning and organizing. "Around that time of puberty, people start specializing," he says. "They start deciding, 'this is what I'm going to be good at, whether it be sports or academics or art or music.' All the life choices, even though they are still there, start getting whittled away, and we have to start . . . focusing on what makes us unique and special."[50] Eating properly and getting plenty of exercise during the teen years can affect the brain's ability to sculpt itself and develop special talents in particular areas. Diet provides the brain with the raw materials that it needs to build new cells and make new connections.

Not only is the teenage brain still growing, but so is the rest of the body. Teenagers gain about half of their adult weight in their

Fourth graders in Virginia choose healthy foods for lunch. Young people need nutrients for growing bones, teeth, and hair. Food also provides the raw materials needed for brain development.

teen years. Marcie Schneider, the director of adolescent medicine at Greenwich Hospital in New York, says that teens should expect to gain as much as 10 to 15 pounds (4.5 to 6.8 kg) every year. "They need tons of extra calories," she says. "You need to gain before you grow, and that slight weight gain at the beginning of puberty is money in the bank."[51] Obese teens may not need to gain weight year by year, and they may need to limit calories in order to lose weight, but while they do so, they have to be careful to get enough nutrients to allow their bodies and brains to continue to grow and develop.

The Role of Exercise

Even more important than diet, according to many doctors, is getting plenty of exercise. Losing weight through exercise is much safer for young people than dieting. Exercise does not carry the risk of preventing the body from getting important nutrients, as dieting does. In fact, exercise helps blood to circulate to the brain, bringing it more oxygen. Exercise also helps the body in other ways. First, it helps build muscle, and muscle tissue, even at rest, burns more calories than fat tissue does. Exercise also makes the heart stronger and lowers blood pressure. Researchers believe that exercise can reduce an obese person's risk of heart disease even if he or she does not lose weight. In addition, studies show that exercise can reduce insulin resistance in obese children.

Exercise also causes the body to release hormones that improve mood and make a person feel happy. By improving mood, exercise can also reduce emotional eating. Because it helps the body overall to be stronger, more flexible, and to feel better emotionally   and because it is fun—exercise can improve the quality of life for obese children and teens, even if they do not lose weight.

Starting Slowly with Exercise

It can be difficult, however, for an obese child or teenager to begin an exercise program. An obese young person might get short of breath during aerobic exercise or have painful joints that limit his or her range of motion. Experts advise obese young people to see a pediatrician before beginning an exercise program and to start slowly. Some obese kids reach their limit after just five minutes of exercise. By that time, they are breathing fast, their faces are red, and their muscles hurt. Studies show that exercising regularly is beneficial, though, even if kids start with five minutes at a time and build up their exercise level by adding more time as they get stronger.

It helps to find an activity that feels good and is gentle on the joints. Often children start by swimming regularly or attending a water aerobics class. Exercising in water is often more com-

"We have kids scoop out spoons of Crisco and put it on a plate. Then they can really see how much fat they're consuming when they eat that hamburger."[49]

— Cindy Zedeck, nutritionist.

Gastric Bypass Surgery

For teenagers who cannot lose weight through diet and exercise, doctors have begun to offer another option: gastric bypass surgery, commonly known as stomach stapling. In this procedure, surgeons actually staple the top part of the stomach together, reducing the usable part of the stomach to the size of a walnut. Food goes directly from the walnut-size stomach to the small intestine, bypassing the rest of the stomach and the first section of the small intestine. After the surgery, patients must stick to a diet of less than 1,200 calories a day for the rest of their lives.

Jade Haycraft of Memphis, Tennessee, had gastric bypass surgery at age 15. She was 5 feet 4 inches tall (163cm) and weighed 367 pounds (166.5kg), and she had tried to lose weight many times. Her BMI was nearly 63 (for an adult, obesity begins with a BMI of 30). Jade's surgery went so well that by the time she was 16, she had lost more than 100 pounds (45.4kg). She lost enough weight to return to school. "I just want it to feel normal," she said at the time.

Jade's doctor first recommended surgery when she was 13. But most doctors prefer not to do gastric bypass surgery on teenagers. One out of every 200 patients dies because of the surgery.

Quoted in Mary Powers, "After the Knife: Jade Takes Chance on Obesity Surgery at 15 to Find Out How 'Normal' Feels," *Memphis Commercial Appeal*, January 1, 2006.

fortable for people with painful joints. Children may also begin by taking short walks and moving at a slow to moderate speed. Some obese children like to ride an exercise bike, but they turn the resistance level on the bike down to zero until they build up some strength. Even gentle exercise can help obese kids to build up strength over time. Nine-year-old Hannah Riley, who began exercising while also following the traffic light diet, could not play on the monkey bars at her school when she first began trying to lose weight. "She couldn't lift her own weight,"[52] her mother told a reporter. But after four months, Hannah reported: "I think I like exercising. I can't wait till recess or lunch so I can go run and play with my friends. I like the playground, the [slide] and the monkey bars."[53]

Emotional Support

Support from family and friends is crucial for anyone trying to lose weight. But for young people, who are experiencing all kinds of new feelings and whose bodies are changing dramatically, support is key. Doctors point out that obese children may experience extreme levels of stress because they are so often teased and treated as if they were lazy or stupid. Helping an obese child to sustain a healthy sense of self-esteem should be the first goal of any weight loss program.

Weight loss counselors also try to help young people to recognize the triggers that might cause emotional eating. "We teach them how to recognize hunger or other feelings that prompt them to eat," says Mongiello, who works at St. Charles Hospital in Port Jefferson, New York. "If they understand their feelings they can ask for what they really want. It isn't always food. They may just want mom to take them to visit a friend or to play a game with them."[54] The program at St. Charles Hospital also provides young people with support groups, so that they can talk with their peers about the process of losing weight. In a group setting, kids can also rehearse different ways to respond to teasing and bullying and have the chance to find out that other kids, too, are coping with the same problems.

Having a support group to talk to also gives obese kids a chance to find out how hard it is for other kids to lose weight or to keep it off once they have lost it. Studies show that it is very difficult for any person, child or adult, to lose weight once he or she has gained it. Many obese children and adults lose weight only to gain it back again. Kids who struggle to

"We teach them how to recognize hunger or other feelings that prompt them to eat. If they understand their feelings they can ask for what they really want. It isn't always food."[54]

— Lorraine Mongiello, nutritionist at St. Charles Hospital in Port Jefferson, New York.

lose weight, or who regain it later, may feel as if the weight gain is a personal failure. They may not realize that sometimes genetics, family environment, and other issues may combine to make losing weight particularly hard in certain cases.

Good weight loss programs for kids work with family members, too, encouraging them to be careful not to give children the impression that they are valued only for the amount of weight they manage to lose and keep off. The plan to reverse obesity and lose all the extra pounds is a quest that may or may not come to pass—and obese children need to know that they have their parents' support whether or not they are able to lose weight. They need to know that their parents want them to be happy—no matter what they weigh. For example, 14-year-old Emily weighs 250 pounds (113.4kg). "I probably would calm down a great deal," says mother Lisa Williams, "if Emily grows up and finds love and a wonderful partner and actually likes what she does and is basically happy, even if she never gets as thin as she should be."[55]

Successful Weight Loss

Can childhood obesity be reversed? Not all obese children and teenagers are able to lose weight and keep it off. If it proves too difficult to lose weight, they can at least eat healthfully and exercise regularly. By doing so, they may be able to avoid many of the usual health risks of obesity. But many kids do manage to lose weight, and when they do, their health often improves dramatically. Taylor S. weighed 250 pounds (113.4kg) before starting a weight loss program. "I didn't want to die in my 40s because of my eating habits,"[56] she admitted. Taylor lost 100 pounds (45.4kg) in 2 years. Angel W. weighed 240 pounds (109kg) and had high blood pressure. She managed to bring her blood pressure down to normal by losing 65 pounds (29.5kg).

Obese kids can succeed in losing weight. But the best option, doctors say, is to prevent obesity by making sure that kids eat healthfully and exercise from the very start.

"I probably would calm down a great deal if Emily grows up and finds love and a wonderful partner and actually likes what she does and is basically happy, even if she never gets as thin as she should be."[55]

— Lisa Williams, mother.

FACTS

- Seventy percent of obese teenagers never lose their excess weight.

- Experts believe that young people can lose weight slowly just by reducing the amount of time they spend watching TV. They recommend watching 30 minutes less each day.

- Boys are more likely than girls to spend large amounts of time in front of a television or computer screen. Girls are more likely than boys to do other sedentary activities, like reading or doing homework.

- A 2009 study showed that obese kids can lose weight and keep it off for at least six months if their families make lifestyle changes.

- Each additional hour of sleep a child gets reduces his or her risk of obesity by 9 percent, according to a 2008 sleep study.

CHAPTER FIVE

Can Childhood Obesity Be Prevented?

Two Arkansas politicians, Republican governor Mike Huckabee and Democrat and former president Bill Clinton, began traveling the country together in 2005. They had decided to work together on a different kind of campaign—a campaign to educate the public about the dangers of childhood obesity. They hoped to inspire people to make nutrition and physical activity of children a priority in towns and cities all across the country.

"Without some intervention, this is the first generation of young Americans, being born today, who are expected to have a shorter life span than their parents or grandparents,"[57] warned Huckabee. "The bottom line is we've got too many kids overweight, and they're walking time bombs,"[58] agreed Clinton.

Educating the Public

Huckabee and Clinton each have their own history of weight problems. When they talk to schools and community groups, each tells his story. At a presentation at a New York City elementary school, Clinton told children that he used to be an obese child. When he was 15, he explained, he was 5 feet 9 inches tall (175.3cm) and weighed 210 pounds (95.3kg). "I was the fat band boy,"[59] he said. Clinton blamed his obesity on his love for fast food and sugar.

In 2004 Clinton had quadruple bypass heart surgery after doctors found that he had extensive blockages in the arteries leading away from the heart. The surgery and the realization that he could have died became the motivation for him to join the campaign against childhood obesity. Clinton's advice to schoolchildren was simple—watch out for foods that are high in fat and high in sugar. "If young children ate 45 fewer calories a day," he reflected, "they would lose two pounds per year and be 20 pounds lighter when they graduated high school."[60]

Like Clinton, Huckabee likes to share his history of obesity. He used to weigh around 300 pounds (136kg) but finally realized he could not continue that way. He invited a University of Arkansas professor of medicine to develop a weight loss plan for him; following the plan religiously, he lost 110 pounds (50kg). Since then Huckabee has become intensely interested in good health. He spearheaded the campaign to screen Arkansas children at school and send letters reporting their BMI home to parents. He is also trying to come up with a plan to make food stamps more valuable if they are spent on healthy foods such as fruits and vegetables.

Clinton and Huckabee's message is reaching local communities. Over the last decade advocacy groups have formed all over the country. Many groups focus on improving nutrition in school cafeterias and making sure that children have a chance to exercise at school. Some groups are concentrating on educating children about healthy food choices and putting more comprehensive labels on foods. Other groups are lobbying state and local government to change laws regarding vending machines in schools, or to get funding to build safe sidewalks so that children can walk to and from school.

"The bottom line is we've got too many kids overweight, and they're walking time bombs."[58]

— Former president Bill Clinton.

Safe Routes to School

Parents in Marin, California, wanted their children to be able to walk or bike to school. But access to one of the elementary schools was over the old Manor Circle Bridge, which parents did not think was safe. "Bicyclists and walkers take their lives into their hands when they use the old bridge,"[61] said Marin resident Wendy Kallins. The bridge had lots of curves and no sidewalks or bike lanes. Parents felt their kids should be able to walk or ride to school. They knew their children needed exercise; experts say that children need about an hour of activity each day and that

Sugar-Sweetened Beverages

The biggest source of sugar in the diets of American children is soda. Teenage girls drink about 36 grams of sugar a day in soda, while teenage boys drink about 58 grams. How does drinking sweet beverages, like soda, affect a child's risk of obesity? Investigators from Boston's Children's Hospital and the Harvard School of Public Health decided to find out. They studied 548 6th and 7th graders from public schools in Massachusetts, tracking how much soda they drank every day. They also kept track of each child's BMI.

During the 21 months that the study lasted, the children drank more soda every day. Every time the children increased their soda consumption by a full serving above their own daily average, their odds of becoming obese rose by 1.6 times. "It is not uncommon for teenagers to receive 500 to 1000 calories per day from sugar-sweetened drinks," warned David Ludwig. Ludwig is the director of the Optimal Weight for Life Program at Children's Hospital in Boston. He went on, "These drinks may be easy to over-consume, because calories in liquid form seem to be . . . less filling than calories in solid form."

Quoted in Harvard School of Public Health, "Study Finds Increased Consumption of Sugar-Sweetened Beverages Promotes Childhood Obesity," press release, February 15, 2001.

walking or riding to and from school is exercise. If children spend 20 minutes walking to school, 20 minutes walking home, and 20 minutes running around at recess, then they have added an hour of exercise 5 days a week.

People in the community learned about a national program called Safe Routes to School. The program helps communities to set up safe walking and biking routes that children can use to get to school. Kallins and other Marin parents had already organized their own Safe Routes to School group in 2000. They had increased Marin's percentage of walkers to 21 percent of Marin students and the number of children biking to school to 38 percent. But many parents still worried about the old bridge.

Then Kallins and the others started lobbying for a bridge that children could use safely. They raised $640,000 for the new bridge—a bridge just for pedestrians and bicyclists. Once the bridge was in place, many more schools joined the program. Almost every elementary, middle, and high school in Marin is accessible through one of the Safe Routes now. Even a few preschools are participating.

The national Safe Routes to School program has become a model for programs all over the country. Community initiatives like the Marin Safe Routes to School program are becoming more common. But not all communities build new routes or add new infrastructure, such as roads, traffic lights, and stop signs. In some neighborhoods, parents have formed a walking club, or "walking school bus." A walking school bus is a group of parents and children who walk to school together to stay safe. The walking school bus always leaves at the same time, follows the same route, and makes regularly scheduled stops to pick up other kids on the way. Like the Safe Routes to School program, the walking school bus provides built-in exercise for children every school day.

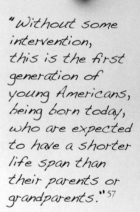

"Without some intervention, this is the first generation of young Americans, being born today, who are expected to have a shorter life span than their parents or grandparents."[57]
— Arkansas governor Mike Huckabee.

Recess Activity of the Week

At school, recess provides children with another opportunity to be physically active. But research shows that many children are not active enough at recess to make a difference. Recess at many elementary schools involves unstructured playtime, where kids can play with balls, run around, climb on monkey bars, slide down slides, or play games if they wish. But not all schools require children to be physically active during recess. Many children just stand around at recess and talk to friends. Researcher Julie Partridge studied playgrounds in northern Colorado. She noticed that older girls, especially, have a tendency to sit down and talk.

Partridge wondered what kids would do if she gave them more activity options. She started an informal two-school study. At one school, she handed out pedometers to kids at recess so that they could monitor their own activity levels. At the other school, she offered one organized activity per week. One week, the activity consisted of tossing Frisbees at targets. The next week, the activity was working one's way through a circuit and obstacle course. The final week, the activity was playing with jump ropes, hopscotch squares, and hula hoops. Partridge was startled by her findings. Kids were eager to try her activities. "The kids liked all of the stuff we brought, but the jump ropes were a really big hit,"[62] she says.

Building on Partridge's research, a group of physical education teachers decided to start their own childhood obesity program designed to motivate children to move around and be more active during recess. They set up play stations where kids could jump rope, play four square, hopscotch, basketball, soccer, hula hoops, and chase. But they also designed a weekly "Recess Activity of the Week"—a structured activity designed to motivate students to play along. Each week, the activity is different. Sometimes it is a golf course or an obstacle course. Other times it might be mat dancing or a circuit route. To pique student interest, the physical education teachers began announcing to the classroom teachers what the activity would be each week. Students could also check a bulletin board.

The 10-Minute Workout

The federal government also encourages physical activity in the schools through various laws. The Child Nutrition and WIC Reauthorization Act of 2004 requires each elementary school, middle school, or high school that participates in the National School Lunch or Breakfast program to offer children a daily workout in addition to their physical education classes. Most of the programs take kids through five or 10 minutes of jumping jacks, running in place, sit-ups, push-ups, and bicycle pedaling.

Debra Thuma, who teaches in a New York elementary school, remarks that her second graders love the exercise. They exercise before doing their academic work, to make sure that they always have time for exercise during the school day. "I like having it first thing in the morning," said seven-year-old Jessica Marmaroff. "Then . . . you don't have to do a lot of work."[63]

The exercise law has its critics. Some people say that the federal government is getting too involved in details that should be controlled by local school boards. But concern about childhood obesity has won over some of the people who would normally be against government intervention in the details of school life. "I don't like government interfering with eating habits or physical activity habits," says Florida state representative Will Weatherford, "but . . . teachers like these kids going out and running around. And kids who go out and run around and burn off energy actually do better academically."[64]

Elementary school students in New Jersey do jumping jacks during a special fitness program. A daily workout of 5 or 10 minutes in addition to regular physical education classes can improve a student's ability to learn.

School Campaigns

In recent years, hundreds of obesity-related bills have been introduced in state legislatures all around the country. Some of the bills call for changes in food labeling, to make it clearer to consumers what foods are most likely to cause obesity. But most of the legislation is directed at schools, and most of the school legislation is intended to push schools to provide nutritious food, not junk food, in cafeterias and vending machines.

Many states are requiring that schools provide nutritious foods to students. As part of this effort, students at a Wisconsin high school now find milk, water, and fruit juices rather than soda in vending machines. But at least one machine still offers candy and chips.

"I'm the mother of a nine-year-old," said Oklahoma representative Susan Winchester, explaining why she felt that having nutritious foods in public schools was so important. "I know what's eaten at our house. If there's a bad choice available it will be chosen. If there's a candy bar, kids will eat that before broccoli."[65]

The Centers for Disease Control and Prevention reports that 1 out of 5 American schools offers fast food such as burgers and fries in the cafeteria at lunchtime and soda, chips, and candy in vending machines for snacks. Schools that do not have enough money in their budgets are trying to raise money by signing "pouring rights" contracts with soda manufacturers. The contracts give the manufacturers the right to maintain vending machines in the schools.

For example, New York City schools have a contract with Snapple. The contract gives the schools a total of $8 million over the course of 5 years. In addition, the producers of Channel One, a television channel broadcast in 12,000 U.S. schools, gives each school that broadcasts the channel a donation of audiovisual equipment. Between news segments, Channel One broadcasts commercials for

State Laws Addressing Childhood Obesity

With obesity on the rise among America's young people, legislators in some states have adopted laws aimed at addressing this problem. School nutrition programs and physical education programs are two ways that states have tried to control obesity in young people. While not all states have laws requiring these programs, many provide one or the other—or both.

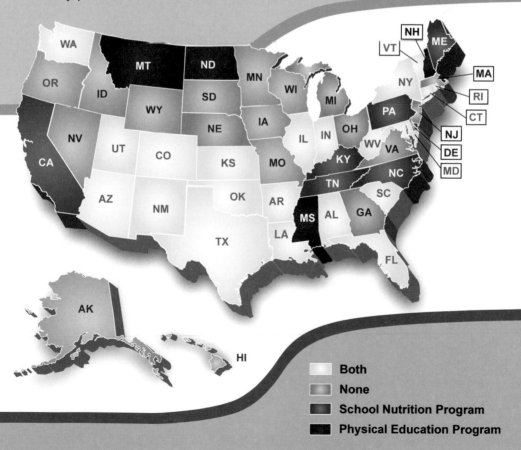

Both
None
School Nutrition Program
Physical Education Program

Source: American Association of Pediatrics, "Childhood Obesity Prevention Legislation, State Legislation Report," 2008. www.aap.org.

McDonald's, Hershey's, Pepsi, Coca-Cola, Frito-Lay, and other manufacturers of empty-calorie foods.

Seventeen states (Arizona, Arkansas, California, Colorado, Illinois, Kansas, Kentucky, Louisiana, Montana, New Hampshire, New Mexico, Oklahoma, Rhode Island, South Carolina, Texas, Virginia, and West Virginia) have passed laws requiring schools to include nutrition in their health curriculum and/or to improve the quality of food served in the cafeteria. School boards in many cities have enacted similar policies. Seattle renegotiated its contract with Coca-Cola, which provides its school vending machines. Under the terms of the new contract, Coca-Cola is only available after school in middle schools and after lunch in high schools. A third of the contents of vending machines must be water or 100 percent fruit juice. And San Francisco's schools have instituted a "no empty calories" policy. Schools were banned from selling junk food—food that is high in calories and low in nutrients.

Critics accused the city of "food fascism," implying that schools were imposing totalitarian rules on students and violating students' rights to choose what they wanted to eat. However, teachers at Aptos Middle School reported better classroom behavior and less litter in their classrooms after the policy began. At Balboa High School, disciplinary suspensions dropped by 50 percent once students had no option but to eat healthy food.

Several states have been considering adding labels to school foods that would explain their nutritional content. In 2005 Colorado enacted a law that requires schools to post nutritional information on foods served in the schools. This information is posted in several different locations that are accessible to parents: at its Web site, on school menus that are sent home, and on bulletin boards inside school buildings.

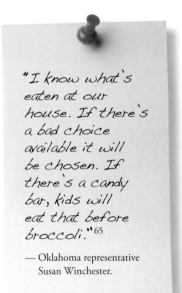

"I know what's eaten at our house. If there's a bad choice available it will be chosen. If there's a candy bar, kids will eat that before broccoli."[65]

— Oklahoma representative Susan Winchester.

Locally Grown School Lunches

Several states have gone a step further and earmarked money to be used to buy local produce to be served in schools. In California, chef Alice Waters pioneered a program that makes school lunches part of the curriculum for students in elementary, middle, and

Modeling Atherosclerosis

A team of science educators in Michigan and New York have worked out a new method for trying to prevent obesity among children. They figured out a way to have students in science classes model the process of atherosclerosis in the arteries. Each pair of students is given clear plastic tubes, modeling clay, and some water that has been dyed red.

First students pour water through the clear tube, observing how easily it flows. Then they add modeling clay to the tube. They add more and more clay, until the hole in the tube is about the size of a pencil point. Then they try to pour the water through again. When students have finished their experiment, teachers start a discussion about what foods are best to eat if kids want to keep their arteries clear. Educators say the best time for kids to do this kind of experiment is in middle school. Young children do not think about how the food they eat affects their bodies. But middle school children are ready to start thinking about the choices they make.

high schools. This way, students can learn about healthy eating habits, and about preventing obesity, while also learning to grow and cook their own food. The program is called Edible Schoolyard. Students who participate plant, care for, and grow fruits and vegetables in a garden on the grounds of their school. The produce is all organic. Students also cook lunches.

Adam Napoleon is a teacher at Career Academy of Piner Olivet High School in Santa Rosa, California, one of the schools that has been testing the sustainable garden program. Napoleon is enthusiastic about the response he sees from his students. "Once the kids try something they've grown themselves but have never eaten before, like Swiss Chard," he says, "they never let me forget it in the next stir fry! And they often come back for seconds."[66]

The sustainable garden plan is slowly spreading from California to the rest of the country. In 2009 schools in Baltimore, Maryland, began planting sustainable gardens. The Baltimore City Public Schools plan to open three student-run restaurants, giving students the opportunity to learn business management skills, as well as learning about nutrition and science. "We want to give the kids the experience of the food from farm to fork," says Baltimore's food service director, Tony Geraci. He goes on, pointing out that nutrition is important in helping young people to be ready to learn, not just to control their weight. "You cannot have the expectation that a teacher can teach if the kid is hungry or jacked up on sugar," Geraci says. "My job is to put healthy kids in front of teachers so that they can teach."[67]

A Black Market in Junk Food

At the same time that school districts are trying to focus on providing healthy food in school lunches, many states are also trying to ban junk food from being sold on school grounds. Colorado requires schools to include nutritious foods in on-campus vending machines and on cafeteria menus and to sell nutritious items for fundraisers. "I think it helps get kids to pay attention to what they eat, what they're putting into their bodies,"[68] says Colorado state representative Alice Madden. Colorado's school vending machines now sell bottled water, juice, nuts, and a few sports drinks.

While parents appreciate Colorado's new policies, not all students do. "It's not a good idea," said 18-year-old Gareth Cameron. "Kids want candy and soda, and they're going to get it one way or another."[69] In some schools, the policy has backfired. A brisk black market in junk food has sprung up in Boulder schools, for example. Two parents, Sue Anne and William, told the *Boulder Weekly* that they had suspected their son, Billy, of dealing drugs. He did not have a job, and he had a lot of cash. When they confronted him, Sue Anne explained, he introduced them to Ralf, another boy from his school. Sue Anne and William were astonished to learn that Billy and Ralf were business partners. Sue Anne remem-

"I don't like government interfering with eating habits or physical activity habits, but . . . teachers like these kids going out and running around. And kids who go out and run around and burn off energy actually do better academically."[64]

— Florida state representative Will Weatherford.

76

bers: "They had this deal worked out where Ralf was buying candy in bulk, very cheaply at Costco, and Billy was selling it. They were marking this stuff up something like ten times the Costco price. And it was selling. They told us it was easy to sell."[70]

Colorado is not the only state to struggle against entrepreneurial kids setting up a black market in candy. After California passed similar legislation, a black market sprang up there, too. Los Angeles high school senior Jennifer Obakhume writes:

> Here's how it works: students buy huge variety boxes of candy and chips or go to Burger King or Starbucks in the morning and then sell their supplies . . . students hide their transactions from stricter teachers when their backs are turned in class. . . . Seniors who get out at noon throw fast food over campus gates to their friends . . . some students even call in pizza orders and have them delivered at the school gate![71]

Faced with a ban on junk food at school, two Colorado students bought and sold candy on their own. The average American teen's love of junk food, including candy and other snacks shown here, is a hard habit to break.

While students responded by setting up a black market, food manufacturers reacted differently. Rather than lose the school market altogether, Coca-Cola and Pepsi began to stock their vending machines with water, milk, and juice. Cliff Bar was developing a new organic energy bar for kids at the time that California passed its legislation. So the company made sure their new ZBar met state requirements and stamped an "SB19 compliant" logo on the package. (*SB19* refers to California State Senate Bill 19, the legislation that requires nutritious food to be sold in schools.) The company made sure the bar included nutrients such as calcium, iron, and folate, and it left out hydrogenated oils and high fructose corn syrup. A war between the students' black market and the corporate vending machines had begun. But so far, the vending machines have not made any less money as a result of selling healthy foods. Advocates insist that some kids must be eating it.

Critics of the new state and federal policies liken the laws to the government in George Orwell's classic novel *1984*. They argue that food choices should be made at home and that students should have junk food around so that they can learn to make their own choices and have an opportunity to make good ones. Connecticut Senate president Donald Williams, however, has an answer for the critics: "No parent is going to sit down at dinner time and say 'Here's your choice: a chicken breast with broccoli, or ice cream and a Snickers bar. It's up to you as my child to exercise your good sense here.' That's not how parents operate."[72]

> "No parent is going to sit down at dinner time and say 'Here's your choice: a chicken breast with broccoli, or ice cream and a Snickers bar.'"[72]
>
> — Connecticut Senate president Donald Williams.

Figuring Out What Will Work

Researchers do not yet know whether the new campaigns to take empty calories out of schools and provide children with plenty of chances to exercise will actually lower the rate of childhood obesity. To find that out, scholars will have to collect statistics on how kids are doing. They will want to compare, over time, the populations of children who attend schools that have these policies with the populations of children who attend schools that do not have these policies. That way, they can find out if the obesity rate tends to go down when children walk to school or when junk food is banned from the cafeteria.

But scientists do know that eating food that is dense in nutrients will help to prevent children from being malnourished. Getting plenty of exercise will make children stronger. Even if childhood obesity rates do not fall as a result of the new policies, encouraging children to develop habits that make them well-nourished and strong is bound to improve their overall health as they move into adulthood.

FACTS

- Lawmakers who are concerned about obesity have focused on schools because 95 percent of obese children and teenagers are enrolled in public schools.

- In 2005, 17 states passed laws increasing the amount of physical education or physical activity programs that are offered in schools.

- In 2004, Congress passed a law requiring all schools that receive federal money for their school lunch or school breakfast programs to have a wellness policy in place to address students' needs for nutrition and physical activity.

- In 2008, 2,800 schools participated in International Walk to School Day, an event designed to encourage young people to get more exercise by walking to school.

- Doctors and educators have succeeded in building awareness about the health risks of childhood obesity. Between 2000 and 2007, the number of articles about obesity in national newspapers increased from about 8,000 in 2000 to more than 28,000 in 2007.

Related Organizations

American Association of Diabetes Educators

200 W. Madison St.
Chicago, IL 60606
phone: (800) 338-3633
Web site: www.diabeteseducator.org

A resource for diabetes patients trying to manage their diabetes at home. Includes information about advocacy and legislative initiatives related to diabetes.

American Diabetes Association

1701 N. Beauregard St.
Alexandria, VA 22311
phone: (800) 342-2383
Web site: www.diabetes.org

Includes information for diabetes patients and family members. Includes lifestyle tips as well as articles about current legislation and research.

American Dietetic Organization

120 S. Riverside Plaza, Suite 2000
Chicago, IL 60606-6995
phone: (800) 877-1600
Web site: www.eatright.org

The world's largest organization of nutritionists. Offers fact sheets, reading lists, information about National Nutrition Month, the USDA's food pyramid, and resources in Spanish.

American Enterprise Institute for Public Policy Research

1150 Seventeenth St. NW
Washington, DC 20036
phone: (202) 862-5800
fax: (202) 862-7177
Web site: www.aei.org/home

The American Enterprise Institute is a private, nonpartisan, not-for-profit institution dedicated to research and education on issues of government, politics, economics, and social welfare. One of its goals is the strengthening free enterprise. Its Web site includes articles and commentary on childhood obesity.

American Heart Association

7272 Greenville Ave.
Dallas, TX 75231
phone: (800) 242-8721
Web site: www.americanheart.org

Offers basic information about heart disease, such as warning signs of a heart attack, nutrition/lifestyle ideas, and information about children and heart disease.

American Obesity Association

8630 Fenton St., Suite 814
Silver Spring, MD 20910
phone: (301) 563-6526
fax: (301) 563-6595
Web site: www.obesity.org

Also known as the Obesity Society. Offers fact sheets, articles, and statistics.

Brookings Institution

1775 Massachusetts Ave. NW
Washington, DC 20026
phone: (202) 797-6000
Web site: www.brookings.edu

The Brookings Institution is a nonprofit liberal research and education organization that is involved in research and education on health, economics, government, and other topics. Its Web site includes a variety of position papers and policy statements about childhood obesity.

Campaign to End Obesity

805 Fifteenth St. NW, Suite 650
Washington, DC 20005
phone: (202) 466-8100
Web site: http://obesitycampaign.org

A national nonprofit organization dedicated to reducing obesity in the general population (not just among children). Offers sheets on obesity and press releases about legislative initiatives.

Kaiser Family Foundation

2400 Sand Hill Rd.
Menlo Park, CA 94025
phone: (650) 854-9400
fax: (650) 854-4800
Web site: www.kff.org

The Kaiser Family Foundation is a nonprofit, nonpartisan private foundation that provides facts, information, and analysis to policymakers, the media, the health care community, and the public. A variety of surveys, fact sheets, studies, and other information on childhood obesity can be found on its Web site.

National Association for Health and Fitness

c/o Be Active New York State
65 Niagara Sq., Room 607
Buffalo, NY 14202
phone: (716) 583-0521
fax: (716) 851-4309
Web site: www.physicalfitness.org

Includes news about legislative fitness initiatives and a link to the physical inactivity cost calculator at East Carolina University.

National Center for Safe Routes to School

730 Martin Luther King Jr. Blvd., Suite 300
Chapel Hill, NC 27599-3430
phone: (866) 610-7787
Web site: www.saferoutesinfo.org

The Web site of the national umbrella organization for state and local Safe Routes to School groups. Offers information about how to start a Safe Routes to School group, as well as forums where members of new and established groups can ask each other questions and offer support.

National Childhood Obesity Foundation

11 Hathaway Rd., Suite 1A
Marblehead, MA 01945
phone: (781) 639-0048
Web site: www.ncof.org

A national nonprofit organization dedicated to educating the public about childhood obesity. Offers articles that have been published in the mainstream press and a free newsletter for kids that provides monthly nutritional information, weight loss tips, and exercise ideas.

Shaping America's Youth

120 NW Ninth Ave., Suite 216
Portland, OR 97209-9221
phone: (800) 279-9221
fax: (503) 273-8778
Web site: www.shapingamericasyouth.org

A resource with links to programs all across the United States that are dedicated to providing education about nutrition and physical fitness for young people.

For Further Research

Books

N.M. Jimerson, *Childhood Obesity.* Detroit: Lucent, 2008. Part of Lucent's Diseases and Disorders series, a general overview of the childhood obesity epidemic.

Martin S. Kipsky, *American Medical Association Guide to Preventing and Treating Heart Disease.* Hoboken, NJ: Wiley, 2008. Basic information about how to recognize heart disease and how it can be treated.

Wendy Murphy, *Weight and Health.* Minneapolis: Twenty-first Century, 2008. Includes personal stories, statistics, and information about trends related to nutrition and obesity.

Kimberly Nix, *Kids Under Construction: Simple Solutions to Help Fight Childhood Obesity.* Atlanta: Asta, 2008. A handbook for families that is aimed at preserving the self-esteem of obese children.

Elizabeth Poskitt, *Managing Childhood Obesity.* New York: Cambridge University Press, 2008. Explains a variety of approaches for changing diet and exercise.

Scott Strother, *The Adventurous Book of Outdoor Games: Classic Fun for Daring Boys and Girls.* Chicago, IL: Sourcebooks, 2008. An encyclopedia of outdoor games that can be played at recess or during gym class.

Internet Sources

Child Development Institute, "Good Nutrition for Kids and Teens." www.childdevelopmentinfo.com/health_safety/nutrition.shtml.

Mayo Clinic, "Childhood Obesity." www.mayoclinic.com/health/childhood-obesity/DS00698.

Office of the Surgeon General, "Overweight in Children and Adolescents." www.surgeongeneral.gov/topics/obesity/calltoaction/fact_adolescents.htm.

Web Sites

Healthy Youth! Health Topics: Childhood Obesity, Centers for Disease Control and Prevention (www.cdc.gov/Healthy Youth/obesity/index.htm). Healthy Youth! is the arm of the Centers for Disease Control and Prevention devoted to children's health. This page includes links to statistics and articles about childhood obesity, national nutrition and obesity education standards, and articles about school success stories.

MedlinePlus: Obesity in Children (www.nlm.nih.gov/medline plus/obesityinchildren.html). Includes links to articles appropriate for different reading levels. The "Basics," "Learn More," and "Reference Shelf" sections provide basic information, while the "Clinical Trials," "Journal Articles," and "Research" sections are only appropriate for advanced readers.

Overweight and Obesity, KidsHealth (http://kidshealth.org/parent/general/body/overweight_obesity.html). Includes articles directed at parents, children, and teenagers, resources about nutrition and exercise, and resources for calculating BMI and ideal weight.

Source Notes

Introduction: A Silent Epidemic

1. Quoted in Holly Yan, "Family Seeks Answers in Boy's Death," *Dallas Morning News*, October 6, 2006. www.dallasnews.com.

2. Quoted in Associated Press, "Boy Dies in Gym Class," October 6, 2006. http://boybuzz.com.

3. Nasser Hasnain, interview with the author, May 22, 2009.

4. Quoted in Walt Larimore, Sherri Flynt, and Steve Halliday, *Super Sized Kids*. New York: Center Street, 2005, p. 14.

5. Hasnain interview.

6. Quoted in Larimore, Flynt, and Halliday, *Super Sized Kids*, p. 13.

7. Quoted in Larimore, Flynt, and Halliday, *Super Sized Kids*, p. 50.

Chapter One: What Are the Origins of Childhood Obesity?

8. Quoted in Harriet Brown, "Well Intentioned Food Police May Create Havoc with Children's Diets," *New York Times*, May 30, 2006. www.nytimes.com.

9. Quoted in Jodi Kantor, "As Obesity Fight Hits Cafeteria, Many Fear a Note from School," *New York Times*, January 8, 2007. www.nytimes.com.

10. Quoted in Elizabeth Weil, "Heavy Questions," *New York Times Magazine*, January 2, 2005. www.nytimes.com.

11. Quoted in Weil, "Heavy Questions."

12. Antoinette Ellis-Williams, "Hop Scotch, Marbles, and Dodge Ball: What Happened to Child's Play?" *NJ.com*, April 18, 2009. www.nj.com.

13. Ellis-Williams, "Hop Scotch, Marbles, and Dodge Ball."

14. Quoted in Amy Winterfield, "What's for Lunch? When's Recess? The Fight Against Obesity Makes Its Way into Schools," *State Legislatures*, December 2005, p. 32.

15. Quoted in Sheba Wheeler, "Schools Bending Traditions to Boost CSAP Scores," *Denver Post*, December 29, 2002. www.susanohanian.org.

16. Quoted in Steven Rosenberg, "Schools Cut Time for Eating, Playing: Officials Say Aim Is to Raise Scores," *Boston Globe*, November 7, 2004. www.boston.com.

Chapter Two: How Serious a Problem Is Childhood Obesity?

17. Quoted in Ginger Thompson, "With Obesity in Children Rising, More Get Adult Type of Diabetes," *New York Times*, December 14, 1998. www.nytimes.com.

18. Quoted in Thompson, "With Obesity in Children Rising, More Get Adult Type of Diabetes."

19. Quoted in Pam Belluck, "Child Obesity Seen as Warning of Heart Disease," *New York Times*, November 11, 2008. www.nytimes.com.

20. Quoted in Karen Goldberg Goff, "Obesity Weighs Heavily on Young," *Washington Times*, April 25, 2004, p. DO1.

21. Quoted in CBS News, "Metabolic Syndrome Common in Obese Children," June 25, 2008. www.cbsnews.com.

22. Quoted in CBS News, "Metabolic Syndrome Common in Obese Children."

23. Quoted in RedOrbit, "Obese Children Break More Bones," November 23, 2005. www.redorbit.com.

24. Quoted in RedOrbit, "Obese Children Break More Bones."

25. Quoted in Melissa McNamara, "Study Links Obesity to Early Puberty," *CBS Evening News*, March 5, 2007. www.cbsnews.com.

26. Quoted in Sylvia Rimm, *Rescuing the Emotional Lives of Overweight Children*. Emmaus, PA: Rodale, 2004, p. 146.

27. Quoted in Phil McKenna, "Childhood Obesity Brings Early Puberty for Girls," *New Scientist*, March 5, 2007. www.newscientist.com.

28. Quoted in McNamara, "Study Links Obesity to Early Puberty."

29. Quoted in Southern Poverty Law Center, "Tolerance in the News: Sizing Up Weight-Based Discrimination," May 3, 2002. www.tolerance.org.

30. Quoted in Helen Briggs, "Tackling Child Obesity in Britain," BBC News, September 11, 2003. http://news.bbc.co.uk.

31. Gary Foster et al., "Primary Care Physicians' Attitudes About Obesity and Its Treatment," *Obesity Research*, October 2003, p. 1,168.

32. Quoted in Carey Goldberg, "Fat People Say an Intolerant World Condemns Them on First Sight," *New York Times*, November 5, 2000. www.nytimes.com.

33. Quoted in BBC News, "I Felt Sick When I Looked in the Mirror." http://news.bbc.co.uk.

34. Quoted in Rimm, *Rescuing the Emotional Lives of Overweight Children*, p. 44.

35. Quoted in Dinitia Smith, "Demonizing Fat in the War on Weight," *New York Times*, May 1, 2004. www.nytimes.com.

36. Quoted in Smith, "Demonizing Fat in the War on Weight."

Chapter Three: What Are the Causes of Childhood Obesity?

37. Quoted in Betty Ann Bowser, "Obese Children," *Online News Hour*, PBS, May 1, 2001. www.pbs.org.

38. Quoted in Salynn Boyles, "Nature Trumps Nurture in Child Obesity," MedicineNet, February 11, 2008. www.medicine net.com.

39. Quoted in Anne Harding, "Family Lifestyle Equals Genes in Obesity Risk," Reuters, December 10, 2008. www.reuters.com.

40. Quoted in Susan Okie, *Fed Up! Winning the War Against Childhood Obesity*. Washington, DC: Joseph Henry, 2005, p. 139.

41. Quoted in Okie, *Fed Up!*, p. 139.

42. Quoted in Joy Alter Hubel, "Losing Weight and Gaining Self-Esteem," *New York Times*, August 3, 1997. www.nytimes.com.

43. Quoted in Jennifer Lee, "Child Obesity Is Linked to Chemicals in Plastics," *New York Times*, April 17, 2009. http://cityroom.blogs.nytimes.com.

Chapter Four: Can Childhood Obesity Be Reversed?

44. Quoted in Abby Ellin, *Teenage Waistland*. New York: Public Affairs, 2005, p. xxxiii.

45. Quoted in Ellin, *Teenage Waistland*, p. 38.

46. Quoted in Ellin, *Teenage Waistland*, p. 40.

47. Quoted in Marek Fuchs, "County Lines: Young, Obese, and Hopeful," *New York Times*, April 28, 2002. http://www.nytimes.com.

48. Quoted in Carin Rubinstein, "Today's Kids Turn Off Fitness," *New York Times*, October 7, 1990. www.nytimes.com.

49. Quoted in Patti Neighmond, "Kids Learn to 'Red Light' Bad Food," NPR, November 2, 2006. www.npr.org.

50. Quoted in *Frontline*, "Inside the Teenage Brain: Interview; Jay Giedd," PBS, 2002. www.pbs.org.

51. Quoted in Tina Kelley, "Am I Too Fat?" *New York Times*, April 4, 2004. www.nytimes.com.

52. Quoted in Neighmond, "Kids Learn to 'Red Light' Bad Food."

53. Quoted in Neighmond, "Kids Learn to 'Red Light' Bad Food."

54. Quoted in Hubel, "Losing Weight and Gaining Self-Esteem."

55. Quoted in Ellin, *Teenage Waistland*, p. xxix.

56. Quoted in Jane Brody, "104 Teenagers Who Are Role Models for Weight Loss," *New York Times*, January 16, 2007. www.nytimes.com.

Chapter Five: Can Childhood Obesity Be Prevented?

57. Quoted in Karen Tumulty, "The Politics of Fat," *Time*, March 19, 2006. www.time.com.

58. Quoted in CNN.com, "Clinton: 'I Was a Fat Band Boy,'" August 7, 2005. www.cnn.com.

59. Quoted in CNN.com, "Clinton."

60. Quoted in Lawrence Altman, "Clinton Joins Fight Against Child Obesity," *New York Times*, May 4, 2005. www.nytimes.com.

61. Quoted in Mark Prada, "New Bridge Promises Safety for School Children," *Marin Independent Journal*, May 2, 2007. www.marinij.com.

62. Quoted in *Southern Spotlight*, "Researcher Studies Kids' Activity Levels at Recess," April 18, 2007. http://spotlight.siu.edu.

63. Quoted in Paul Vitello, "When Second Graders Run Wild, with Federal Approval," *New York Times*, June 9, 2007. www.nytimes.com.

64. Quoted in Amy Winterfield, "What's for Lunch? When's Recess? The Fight Against Obesity Makes Its Way into Schools," *State Legislatures*, December 2005, p. 32.

65. Quoted in Winterfield, "What's for Lunch?" p. 32.

66. Quoted in Nicole Zimmerman, "School Garden Network Supports Local Programs," *West County Gazette*, January 21, 2009. www.westcountygazette.com.

67. Quoted in Jane Black, "Radical in the Lunch Line," *Washington Post*, May 6, 2009. www.washingtonpost.com.

68. Quoted in Winterfield, "What's for Lunch?" p. 32.

69. Quoted in Wendy Laugeson, "Sugar High," *Boulder Weekly*, November 8–14, 2007. www.boulderweekly.com.

70. Quoted in Laugeson, "Sugar High."

71. Jennifer Obakhume, "Black Market for Junk Food," Youth Radio, November 6, 2005. www.youthradio.org.

72. Quoted in Joseph Popiolkowski, "First 'State Law Compliant' Snack Food Launched," *Health Care News*, January 2007. www.heartland.org.

Index

Martin, Molly, 46–47

McDonald, David, 25

medications, for diabetes/high blood pressure, increase in number of children taking, 39

Messiah, Sarah, 32

metabolic rate, 57

metabolic syndrome, 32–33
  prevalence in obese children, 39

Miller-Kovach, Karen, 54

minorities
  risk of diabetes in, 30
  as target of public attacks on obesity, 35

Molina, Stephanie, 8

Mongiello, Lorraine, 49, 63

Napoleon, Adam, 75

National Association for Sport and Physical Education, 20

National Educational Association, 35

National Heart, Lung, and Blood Institute, 35

Obakhume, Jennifer, 77

obesity
  in adults, increase in prevalence of, by state, 43 (map)
  emotional eating and, 49

exposure to toxins and, 50

genetic role in, 41, 42, 44, 52

link between viruses and, 50–51

among Pima people, 44–46

as political issue, 35

television viewing and, 47–49

twins studies on, 41–42, 46–47

See also health risks, of obesity

Pacific Islanders, 51

Partridge, Julie, 69–70

phthalates, 50

physical education
  decline in teens taking daily classes of, 26
  number of states increasing, 79
  schools have cut back on, 23–25

Pima people (Akimel O'odham), obesity among, 44–46, 48, 51

poverty
  empty-calorie foods and, 19–20
  as risk factor for obesity, 26

puberty, early onset of, 34

About the Author

Bonnie Juettner is a writer and editor of children's reference books and educational videos. She is also a mother of two and a lifelong vegetarian. This book brings together two topics that particularly interest her—children and nutrition.